INTRODUCTION

F athers and mothers, husbands and wives, sons and daughters—the men and women of the Bible each have a story to
tell. And between the covers of this book, you'll find the intriguing stories of more than one hundred individuals, in order of their
appearance in the Bible. From Adam and Eve to Lydia, Mark,
Peter, and Paul, these stories will inspire and encourage you as you
live out your own story.

MEN AND WOMEN OF THE BIBLE

More Than One Hundred Intriguing Stories

DAN HARMON
COLLEEN L. REECE

BARBOUR
PUBLISHING

© 2003 by Barbour Publishing, Inc.

ISBN 1-58660-939-4

Cover image © PhotoDisc, Inc.

Previously published as *Men of the Bible* by Dan Harmon © 1997 and *Women of the Bible* by Colleen L. Reece © 1998.

Published by Barbour Publishing, Inc., P.O. Box 719, Uhrichsville, Ohio 44683, www.barbourbooks.com

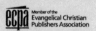 Member of the
Evangelical Christian
Publishers Association

Printed in the United States of America.
5 4 3 2 1

ADAM

GENESIS 2:4–5:5

Adam was the first human, formed from dust and given God's own breath of life. He was placed in a beautiful garden God had planted in Eden. The Lord made Adam the caretaker of His garden and surrounded him with many wonderful plants for beauty and for food. God brought to Adam all the animals He had created, and Adam named them. Adam was free to enjoy this lovely garden. Only one restriction was placed on him: "Do not eat from the tree of the knowledge of good and evil," God warned. This tree was at the center of the garden.

God did not want Adam to live alone, so He put the man into a deep sleep, removed one of his ribs, and created a woman from the rib. He made the woman Adam's wife. Adam named her Eve.

Sadly Adam and Eve were persuaded by the serpent to eat fruit from the forbidden tree. This may be the most famous story in the Bible. It resulted in alienation between God and Adam and Eve and all their descendants. Adam and Eve were evicted from the garden and had to work the soil to grow their food.

This first sin led to the avalanche of sin that characterizes the whole human race. In fact, Adam and Eve's son Cain jealously murdered his own brother. Soon the world was so wicked the Lord was compelled to destroy it with a great flood. God allowed humanity to continue by preserving Noah and his family, but their descendants quickly returned to the errant ways established by Adam and Eve. It would take the crucifixion of Jesus Christ many centuries later to atone for Adam's original sin.

EVE

GENESIS 2–4

Coolness patterned the garden into a mosaic of sunlight and shade. Soft footfalls announced the presence of One walking amidst trees and flowers. A voice, low but indescribably sweet, called, "Adam, where art thou?"

Trembling, the man and woman, formed and breathed into life by the Lord God Almighty, crept out of hiding. "Here, Lord," Adam whispered.

Eve shivered and clutched his arm, seeking strength yet knowing he had none to give the helpmeet God had created from one of Adam's ribs. The look in her husband's face when confronted by his Creator seared Eve's soul and burned like a hot coal that could not be extinguished. Fear. Shame. Regret. Brokenness. More than anything else, it showed her the magnitude of her folly. Why had she listened to the tempter? Worse, why had she caused her sinless husband to transgress God's law by encouraging him to do likewise?

If only they could go back just a few hours! The garden had been beautiful. God said they might eat fruit from all the trees in the garden, save one. If they ate from that tree, they would surely die. Neither Eve nor Adam questioned God.

Then the serpent appeared. "Ye shall not die. God knows that in the day ye eat your eyes shall be opened. Ye shall be as gods, knowing good and evil."

The tree before Eve glowed with beauty, offering food alluring above all others—and something more: wisdom, as the serpent promised. She reached out, took fruit, and ate. How wonderful! She plucked more and ran with it to her husband, who accepted it from her hands.

Innocence vanished. Aware of their nakedness for the first time, they hastily gathered fig leaves and formed aprons to cover themselves. When they heard God walking in the garden, they fled. What had seemed such a little thing at the time turned monstrous in their new knowledge of good and evil.

Eve shuddered, sickened by how easily she had turned away from right and chosen wrong. Half-dazed, she heard Adam explaining to God that first Eve, then he, had eaten the forbidden fruit.

The Lord said to Eve, "What is this that thou hast done?"

Pierced to her innermost being by the sorrow in His voice, she said through dry lips, "The serpent beguiled me, and I did eat." Self-loathing filled her.

God cursed the serpent for what it had done. He condemned the tempter to crawl on its belly and said there would be enmity between him and womanhood forever. Then he turned back to Eve. "I will greatly multiply thy sorrow and thy conception; in sorrow thou shalt bring forth children; and thy desire shall be to thy husband, and he shall rule over thee."

Filled with misery and longing only to escape the presence of the One who had made her, Eve suffered even more when the Lord spoke to Adam. Because he had listened to his wife rather than keeping the commandment of God, he must toil all the days of his life. Thorns and thistles would hinder his work, and only by the sweat of his brow would he be able to bring forth food from the ground now cursed.

God made coats of skins and clothed Adam and Eve. He drove them from the garden of Eden, lest they eat of the tree of life and live forever. Eve sobbed uncontrollably, but cherubim and a turning, flaming sword made it impossible for Adam and her to ever again walk with God in the garden.

Time passed. God's promises remained sure. Adam worked hard, tilling the ground. Eve brought forth children in travail, the mother of all living. Her heart tore with pain until she wondered if she would go mad when her eldest son Cain slew Abel, his younger brother, in a jealous rage.

Sorrow and joy, hard times and pleasant, the years rolled on. At times the lovely garden in which she and Adam once walked with God seemed remote, shrouded by the mist of many years. Yet, as long as she lived, Eve never forgot her agony when she watched Adam face his Maker and recognized what havoc she had brought into the world by listening to the tempter rather than to God.

CAIN AND ABEL

GENESIS 4:1–16, 25

C ain was the oldest son of Adam and Eve. Abel was his brother. Cain farmed the soil, Abel was a shepherd. When they brought the Lord offerings of the fruit of their labors, God was not equally impressed. Cain's gift was a sampling of his crops—the Lord did not bless it. The blessing was reserved for the sacrifice of Abel— the choicest meat from his firstborn lamb.

This angered Cain, and the Lord chastised him for being angry and warned, "If you do well, you will be blessed. But if you do wrong, sin will overtake you." Ignoring the warning, Cain killed his brother in a rage.

Later God asked him, "Where is your brother?"

Cain retorted, "Am I my brother's keeper?"

Of course the Lord already knew what had happened and condemned Cain to a life of endless wandering. Never again would the ground he farmed produce food.

"But I'll be homeless," Cain protested, "easy prey for anyone to kill."

So God placed a mark on Cain to warn people not to harm him. But for Cain, death would have been preferable to a roving existence in exile from the presence of God.

NOAH

GENESIS 5:28–10:32

Judgment was at hand. Since the time of Adam and Eve, humans had multiplied, spread across the earth, and progressively turned away from God. "I am sorry I created them," God said of these violent and wicked people. "I will destroy every living creature on the face of the earth."

Only one man feared and obeyed God. His name was Noah. God told him of His plan to destroy both humans and animals with a great flood. But God gave Noah specific instructions for building an ark in which he, his family, and two each of every living creature would ride out the deluge.

The ark was like a huge barge, one hundred and fifty yards long and three stories high. Noah followed every detail of the Lord's commands, built the ark of strong wood, and sealed it carefully with pitch.

Finally the ark was finished. God gave Noah seven days to gather and board all of the animals. Then He made it rain forty days and nights. The flood rose, covered the lowlands, then the hills, and finally even the highest mountains. The water was so deep that once the rain stopped, five months passed before flood receded and the ark came to rest in the mountains of Ararat. It was many more months before the earth was dry again. Noah waited inside until God told him to leave the ark.

The first thing Noah did was make an offering of one of each of the sacrificial animals that had been in the ark. The Lord was pleased by this offering and promised Noah He never again would destroy every living creature by flood. A rainbow appeared in the sky as a perpetual reminder of this covenant with Noah. God gave Noah dominion over all the animals and plants. Everyone living on the earth today is descended from Noah and his sons Shem, Ham, and Japheth.

ABRAHAM

Generally regarded as the "father of the Jewish nation," Abraham's life is a wondrous example of how God works His will in impossible situations.

The life story of this grand Old Testament patriarch would pale the most intricate plots of Hollywood screenwriters—and it all really happened! God told Abraham to break away from his father's family and go to a new land. God promised to make a great nation of Abraham's descendants and bless them. "I will bless those who bless you and curse those who harm you," the Lord told him. So began the formation and trials of God's chosen people.

There was an unhappy chasm between Abraham and his nephew Lot. But when Lot and his household were captured by a warring kingdom, Abraham and a commando force of three hundred soldiers rescued them. God made a covenant with Abraham and promised that his descendants would be as numerous as the stars in the sky—even though Abraham's wife, Sarah, was too old to bear children. In fulfillment of this promise God gave them a son in their old age. They named him Isaac.

Nowhere was Abraham's obedience so severely tested as in the mountains of Moriah where the Lord commanded him to sacrifice Isaac. Abraham prepared the altar, gathered the wood, lit the fire, bound the unsuspecting youth, and placed him on the altar. Abraham drew a knife and was actually poised to kill his son—so committed was he to God—when an angel of the Lord stayed his hand at the last instant.

Abraham had proven he would keep nothing from the Almighty, not even his cherished son. In return, God reiterated His pledge to make Abraham's descendants as numerous as the stars in the sky and as the grains of sand along the ocean shore.

Sarah lived to be 127, Abraham, 175, and they were buried in a cave in the field of Ephron in Canaan.

LOT

GENESIS 11:31; 12:4; 13:1–14:16; 19:1–38;
LUKE 17:28–30

When God sent Abraham and his wife, Sarah, into the land of Canaan, they were accompanied by Abraham's nephew Lot. In time, Abraham and Lot prospered in the new land. As their flocks grew larger, however, their shepherds quarreled over pastureland. To make peace, Abraham gave Lot his choice of land to settle on, so Lot moved east to the fertile Jordan River valley. There he pitched his tents near Sodom, a city of evil people. Meanwhile, Abraham settled in Canaan.

Intercity warfare soon visited the Jordan Valley, and Lot and his household were taken captive by a conquering army. When Abraham got word of this, he took several hundred men and pursued the marauders. In the aftermath of a brilliant surprise attack, Abraham's men scattered the enemy and rescued Lot and the other captives.

Fifteen years later, Lot found himself in even greater trouble. The cities of Sodom and Gomorrah had become so evil that God planned to destroy them. Lot was sitting near the city gate of Sodom when two men (who were actually angels) approached. Lot insisted that they stay with him and share a meal. After supper they were roused to find that Lot's house was surrounded by all the men of the city. The evil men called for Lot to send the two men outside. The mob had wicked intentions. Lot was afraid for the strangers and to pacify the mob offered to send his two virgin daughters out to them. "Do not harm my guests," he pleaded. Lot's refusal to release the strangers to them angered the would-be molesters. They rushed the door of the house, but the two angels struck them blind!

The angels instructed Lot to take his family and leave immediately because the Lord's destruction of Sodom was imminent. Naturally, Lot's family resisted. The angels had to take Lot, his wife, and his two daughters by the hand and lead them out of the city. As they fled in the predawn hour, God rained fiery sulfur down on the cities of Sodom and Gomorrah, which were consumed together with all their inhabitants. Lot and his family were saved. All except for Lot's wife. She could not resist turning to look back at the destruction of her home. At that very spot she was turned to a pillar of salt.

This sordid story does not end here. After their escape from Sodom, Lot and his two daughters lived in a cave. The daughters worried that they would never be married and have children. So they made their father drunk and slept with him. The two children, which came forth from these incestuous unions, were ancestors of the nations of Moab and Ammon, future enemies of Israel.

SARAI

GENESIS 12, 16–18, 20–21, 23

Hunched and intense, Sarai listened to the remarkable tale her husband Abram related. "The Lord came to me in a vision. He told me He was my shield and my exceeding great reward. I cried to Him, 'Lord, God, what will Thou give me, seeing I go childless? Thou hast given me no seed, and lo, one born in my house is mine heir.' "

" 'This shall not be thine heir,' the Lord said. 'Look now toward heaven and tell the stars, if thou be able to number them. So shall thy seed be.' "

"You believe this to be true?" Sarai tried to keep her words calm, although her heart pounded with doubt.

"Yea, for He showed me many other things."

A ripple of scornful laughter escaped Sarai's lips. "I am an old woman, Abram," she proclaimed. "My childbearing days—if I ever had such—are long past." Bitterness crept into her voice.

"I only know what the Lord has said." Abram rose and departed.

They spoke no more of the matter, but it lay between them, a living thing that permitted Sarai no rest. Why God had restrained her from bearing, she did not know. Why, then, had Jehovah given her husband the vision? Stay. Perhaps it was no vision but the product of Abram's longing for a son.

When Sarai could no longer bear the weight pressing on her, she went to her husband. "Behold now, go in unto my maid; it may be that I may obtain children by her."

Abram hearkened to Sarai's voice. He took the Egyptian maid Hagar to be his wife, and she conceived. At once, Hagar began to despise her mistress.

Sarai saw it. Fury raged within her. Had she not given Hagar to her own husband that God's promise might be fulfilled? Now the younger woman dared set herself up against her mistress. It was unbearable.

"My wrong be upon thee," Sarai upbraided Abram. "I have given my maid into thy bosom, and when she saw she had conceived, I was despised in her eyes: The Lord judge between me and thee." She held her breath, waiting his judgment.

"Behold, thy maid is in thy hand; do to her as it pleaseth thee."

Sarai dealt harshly with Hagar, who fled from her wrath for a time.

When Abram was ninety and nine years old, the Lord appeared and gave him a new name: Abraham. He established an everlasting covenant to be a God unto Abraham and his seed. He also gave Sarai a new name. Henceforth, she would be no longer Sarai but Sarah. She would have a son, who would be called Isaac, and become a mother of nations. Abraham fell upon his face and laughed in his heart. A man have a son at one hundred, with a wife of ninety long years? Never in the history of the world had such a thing happened.

Sarah could not and would not believe she would bear a son in her old age but denied laughing, for she was afraid. When she conceived and began to be great with child, Sarah pondered how such a thing could be. After long, empty years, God had granted her the desire of her heart.

Abraham was a hundred years old when Sarah delivered Isaac, whose name means "laughter." And she said, "God hath made me to laugh, so that all that hear will laugh with me. Who would have said unto Abraham that Sarah should have given children suck? For I have born him a son in his old age."

The child grew, and on the day Isaac was weaned, Abraham made a great feast. Sarah had not conquered her hatred of Hagar. She demanded that Hagar and her son Ishmael be cast out. Sarah rejoiced when the bondwoman and young Ishmael went away into the wilderness, not realizing God would one day make the young man ruler of a nation.

Sarah lived to be a hundred and twenty-seven years old. She never stopped marveling that God had sent a son into her barren life long after hope of such a thing had unfolded its wings and flown away.

ISHMAEL

GENESIS 16; 21:9–21

Ishmael was the son of scheming and jealousy.

Abraham and Sarah were childless. Sarah, frustrated by her barren condition, formulated a solution. She gave Abraham her Egyptian maid Hagar as his wife, so Hagar could bear a child on Sarah's behalf. After she became pregnant, Hagar could not hide her feelings of contempt toward her barren mistress, Sarah. Angrily Sarah mistreated her, and Hagar fled into the wilderness. An angel found her there deeply distressed and admonished her to return to Sarah's service. The angel told her that her unborn son should be called Ishmael, that he would be a wild man, and contend with many people. Yet Ishmael would give Hagar a line of descendants too numerous to count.

So Hagar returned to the house of Abraham and Sarah.

Ishmael was a teenager when God finally gave a son to Abraham and Sarah. With the birth of Isaac, tension mounted within the household. Sarah wanted to make sure their entire inheritance went to her son Isaac, so she demanded that Abraham send Hagar and Ishmael away.

Abraham did not want to do this. He was afraid Hagar and Ishmael would not survive. But the Lord assured him, "Your son Isaac will have your inheritance and continue your lineage, but your son Ishmael also will father a great nation."

Abraham sent the servant woman and her son away with water and bread. Roaming through the wilderness near Beersheba, they soon ran out of food and water. Hagar placed her son in the shade of a bush then stumbled off, so she would not have to see him die.

In the depth of her despair, Hagar was again visited by an angel who led her to a well of water. "Do not worry," the angel said, "Ishmael will survive and become the father of a long line of descendants."

Ishmael grew up to be a great hunter, and his mother found an Egyptian woman for him to marry. He did not receive his father's inheritance, but Ishmael nevertheless was richly blessed as the Lord had promised his mother.

HAGAR

GENESIS 16, 21

I hate being a handmaid, the Egyptian girl Hagar thought. *Especially for one like Sarai. She is old and ugly. I am younger and alive. Why must I serve and obey her?* She pressed her lips together, and her resentful thoughts rushed on. Nothing she did ever proved good enough for her fault-finding mistress. The plight of one who served had never weighed down on her so heavily as right now. Sarai became more demanding with each passing day.

Hagar smothered mirth, fearful of being discovered at the secret listening post where she learned much more than her mistress knew. Abram had just finished relating some impossible dream he called a vision from God.

Sarai's derisive laughter echoed in Hagar's heart. The idea! What kind of God thought a man of Abram's age could father a child? Pah! Her contempt grew. Even if he were able, why would Sarai conceive now when she hadn't in all these years? Hagar shook with silent laughter, but in the following days, she caught a brooding look in her mistress's eyes. She learned Sarai planned to give her handmaid to Abram.

At first the idea repelled Hagar, then cunning rose. A wife, even a second wife, held a more important place than a servant. Even if she never conceived, anything was better than her present position. She shrugged. Her wishes in the matter meant nothing. A handmaid did her mistress's bidding.

When Hagar knew she had conceived, triumph flooded through her. She made no attempt to hide her disdain of Sarai, childless and barren. As carrier of Abram's son and heir, she felt she would also have his protection. She did not. He gave Sarai permission to deal with her as she would. Many a bitter tear Hagar wept before fleeing into the wilderness on the way to Shur. Not until she reached a fountain of water did she stop and wonder what would become of her and her unborn child. There an angel of the Lord found her.

"Whence camest thou? Wither wilt thou go?" he asked.

Rubbing her eyes to make sure she was not dreaming, Hagar replied, "I flee from the face of my mistress Sarai."

The angel told her she must return and submit herself to Sarai. He promised to multiply Hagar's seed exceedingly. He also told her she was with child and would bear a son. "The Lord has heard thy affliction," he said. "Name the child Ishmael"—whom God hears— "because the Lord hath heard thy affliction. And he will be a wild man; his hand against every man, and every man's hand against him."

Hagar returned to Sarai. Ishmael was born when Abram was fourscore and six years old. His delight in his son made up for some of what Hagar suffered from Sarai, who daily grew more resentful of her handmaid and the boy. Things worsened when Ishmael was fourteen and Sarai, now Sarah, delivered then weaned Isaac. What would become of Hagar and Ishmael?

They soon found out. The next morning, Abraham, as he was called, rose early, put bread and a bottle of water on Hagar's shoulder, and sent her away with Ishmael to wander in the wilderness of Beersheba.

When the water was spent, she cast her son under one of the shrubs and went a far distance off. "Let me not see the death of the child." She lifted up her voice and wept.

The angel of God called to Hagar out of heaven. "What aileth thee, Hagar? fear not; for God hath heard the voice of the lad. Arise, lift up the lad, and hold him in thy hand; for I will make him a great nation." God opened Hagar's eyes, and she saw a well of water. She filled the bottle and gave the lad drink, holding the promises of the angel of God deep in her heart.

As Ishmael grew, God was with him. The boy dwelt in the wilderness and became an archer. Hagar took him a wife out of the land of Egypt and great was her joy. Outcasts from the tents of Abraham they might be, yet God had protected her and the child of her body. Twice an angel had promised Ishmael would be a great nation. One day it would come to pass. Blessed be Jehovah!

ISAAC

L aughter was the meaning of his name because his birth brought great rejoicing. He was God's promise to his aged parents, Abraham and Sarah.

Isaac's upbringing was stamped with a unique demonstration of love and obedience to God. His trek into the land of Moriah with Abraham, the building of the altar in the middle of nowhere, the binding of his hands and feet, his placement on the altar, his father's upraised knife—then, in that moment of incredible terror, when the child could neither understand nor believe what was being done to him, came the saving cry of God's angel—"Abraham! Abraham!"

The knife was stayed. "Now I know," the angel told Abraham, "that you love God above all else—even more than your son who is so precious to you."

Isaac's is the earliest love story. Abraham did not want Isaac to marry any of the women in Canaan. He instructed his chief servant to travel east to Abraham's homeland and find a wife for Isaac. "God will send His angel before you," Abraham assured the servant.

The servant took ten camels and many gifts and departed. Outside the city of Haran, he stopped at a spring. This was the end of the day, and the women of the city were coming out to draw water. The servant prayed that God would show him the woman who was to be Isaac's wife. This would be the test: The servant would ask for a drink of water; the woman, if she was the right one, would offer water not only to him but to his camels.

Immediately a beautiful young woman named Rebekah, granddaughter of Abraham's brother Nahor, came to the spring. "Please let me have some water from your jar," the servant said.

"Drink," she said, lowering her jar. Then she drew more water for the camels.

Invited to stay the night with Rebekah's family, the servant told them the story of his mission and of the test at the spring. "It is God's will," agreed Rebekah's father. He asked Rebekah if she would go with the envoy and become Isaac's wife. "I will," she said.

One evening Isaac was walking in the field when he saw the servant returning. With the servant was a young woman who had her face veiled. Isaac married Rebekah and was comforted in his grief after his mother Sarah's death. He loved Rebekah very dearly.

The couple were blessed by God. Isaac became very wealthy. But their twin sons Esau and Jacob were to open a stormy chapter in the history of God's people. The details of their dramatic rivalry are recounted separately in this book. Thankfully, by the time of Isaac's death in Hebron at age 180, Esau and Jacob had reconciled.

LOT'S WIFE

GENESIS 19

Lot, nephew of Abraham, hastened home at eventide and called to his wife, "Make haste! Prepare unleavened bread."

The mistress of the household looked up, startled by his excitement. She caught sight of two strangers entering the house behind him. "Who—?"

Lot lowered his voice. "As I sat at the gate of the city, two angels came to me. I bowed and prayed that they might tarry all night in this, their servant's house. At first they said nay, they would abide in the street, but when I pressed upon them greatly, they agreed."

Angels! The woman's mouth fell open, but she hurried to do her husband's bidding, pressing her daughters into service, as well.

Before the household lay down for the night, the men of Sodom encircled the dwelling place, demanding the strangers be brought to them.

Lot stepped outside and closed the door. He entreated them not to do wickedly. He said, "Behold, I have two daughters which have not known man; let me, I pray you, bring them out unto you, and do ye to them as is good in your eyes: Only unto these men do nothing; for therefore came they under the shadow of my roof."

Anger raged inside his listening wife. Was he mad, to sacrifice his own daughters for the sake of the two sheltered under his roof? If they were indeed angels, could they not protect themselves from the rabble outside the door?

Lot's pleas proved useless. The crowd pressed sore upon Lot and came forth to break the door. Before they could do so, the strangers pulled Lot inside, shut the door, and smote the mob with such blindness they could not find the door.

Weak with relief, Lot's wife sank back to her pallet and clutched a shawl around her. She heard the visitors say, "Hast thou here any besides? son-in-law, and thy sons, and thy daughters, and whatsoever thou hast in the city, bring them out of this place; for we will destroy this, because the cry of them is grown great before the face of the Lord; and the Lord hath sent us to destroy it."

Destroy the city? The listening woman plucked at her shawl with nervous fingers. Lot went out and told his sons-in-law they must get up and leave at once. They laughed and mocked him, refusing to believe the Lord would destroy the city.

In the morning the angels hastened Lot. "Arise, take thy wife, and thy two daughters which are here; lest they be consumed in the iniquity of the city." While Lot lingered, the angels laid hold upon his hand, and his wife and daughters' hands, and led them forth, the Lord being merciful. One angel warned, "Escape for thy life; look not behind thee, neither stay thou in all the plain; escape to the mountain, lest thou be consumed."

Lot pleaded that they might instead flee to a little city that would not be overthrown. The angel agreed and again urged them to make haste.

The sun had risen by the time Lot and his wife entered Zoar. Terrible sounds came from Sodom and Gomorrah, even from the plain and all that grew on the ground. Lot's wife could not stand it. From her position behind her husband, she wailed with grief. Only two of her daughters had been saved. The others had remained in Sodom with their husbands. In her despair, she turned her face toward the way they had come, either ignoring or forgetting the commandment the angel had given not to look back. Fire and brimstone fell from heaven, devouring everything and everyone in its path.

When Lot and his daughters sought the wife and mother who had accompanied them, nothing remained but a pillar of salt.

ABIMELECH

The Hebrew woman Sarah was very beautiful, and Abimelech, king of Gerar, took notice. She had been living in Abimelech's country with Abraham for some time. Abimelech thought they were brother and sister and so brought Sarah into his household to be one of his wives, as was the accepted custom of the time. But Abimelech was a God-fearing man. He was devastated when the Lord came to him in a dream and revealed that Sarah was in fact Abraham's wife!

"But I did not know I was doing wrong!" Abimelech protested. "They both told me they were brother and sister."

Happily, the Lord had not allowed Abimelech to touch Sarah after she had entered his house. "Return Abraham's wife to him," the Lord said. "He is a prophet, and he will pray for you. But if you do not return her, you and everyone in your household will die."

Early the next day, Abimelech told his servants what had happened. He summoned Abraham and demanded to know why the couple had deceived him. Abraham explained: When he and Sarah entered Gerar he was not sure it was a land of God-fearing people. He was afraid some man enticed by Sarah's beauty would kill him in order to obtain her as a wife. So Abraham persuaded Sarah to pose as his sister. She was, after all, his half sister because they had the same father.

Rather than venting his fury against Abraham, Abimelech gave him an offering of livestock, slaves, and money. He gave him the best land in Gerar on which to live. Of course he returned Sarah to him unharmed. Abimelech wanted everyone to know he had not come near Sarah. During the time Sarah was in Abimelech's household, the Lord had made the king impotent. But after Abraham prayed for him, God restored Abimelech to full health.

Abimelech is a notable example of a God-fearing man who, when confronted with his mistake, went out of his way to seek reconciliation with the people he had harmed and, most importantly, reconciliation with the Lord.

REBEKAH

GENESIS 24, 27

The eldest servant of the house of Abraham knelt by a well of water near the city of Nahor in Mesopotamia. Ten laden camels waited nearby. "Oh Lord God of my master, Abraham, I pray thee, send me good speed this day, and show kindness unto my master." He paused. Could he fulfill the oath he had made to his master? Abraham had told him an angel would go before and lead the trusted servant to a kinswoman willing to accompany him to the tents of Abraham and become wife to Abraham's son Isaac. How would a humble servant know her?

He continued, "Behold, I stand here by the well. The daughters of the men of the city come out to draw water. Let it come to pass that the damsel to whom I shall say, 'Let down thy pitcher, that I may drink' and she shall say, 'Drink, and I will give thy camels drink also': Let the same be she that Thou hast appointed for Thy servant Isaac."

Before he had finished speaking, Rebekah, a fair young virgin, went down to the well and filled her pitcher. She curiously eyed the stranger and his well-laden camels. He asked for water, and she gladly gave him her brimming pitcher. "I will also draw water for the camels," she told the stranger. Pitcher after pitcher she drew and poured into the trough so the camels could quench their thirst.

When they finished, the servant gave Rebekah a golden earring of half a shekel weight, two bracelets, and ten shekels' weight of gold. He asked her father's name and if lodging could be had in his house.

"I am daughter of Bethuel, the son of Milcah, which she bare unto Nahor," she proudly announced. "We have both straw and provender enough, and room to lodge in."

Nahor, brother of Abraham! The servant bowed his head and worshipped the Lord, praising Him for His leading.

Rebekah ran and told those of her household concerning the strange encounter. Her brother Laban immediately went for the stranger and welcomed him. While they sat at meat, the servant told everything that had transpired. He told how rich Abraham was in flocks and herds, of servants, silver, gold, and beasts. He related how a son had been born to Sarah in her old age and that Abraham had sent his eldest servant to find a kinswoman to become Isaac's wife.

Rebekah's heart leaped within her, especially when the man confessed he had prayed for God to lead the right woman to the well and had even given the words she should say! Humility at having been selected by God as Isaac's wife filled her, and she breathlessly waited for her family to speak.

"Wilt thou go with this man?" Laban and Bethuel asked Rebekah.

"I will." They blessed her and sent her on her journey.

Rebekah whiled away the weary traveling hours wondering what her husband-to-be would be like. When she first saw Isaac, she found him pleasant to look upon. His eyes held love, and she became his wife.

Twenty barren years later, when Isaac was three score, the Lord blessed Rebekah with twins: Esau, hairy and red, then Jacob. Esau turned to hunting and the field, and Jacob, whom Rebekah loved more, dwelt in the tents. She secretly rejoiced when Esau sold his birthright to his younger brother for bread and a pottage of lentils. Had not Jacob been born with one hand on Esau's heel, symbolizing that he, not his elder brother, should rule?

Isaac grew old. Rebekah's ambitions for Jacob soared. She commanded him to disguise himself as Esau, take the savory meat Isaac loved, and receive the blessing that belonged to the older son. Fear soon replaced her joy. The cheated Esau threatened to kill Jacob, and Rebekah sent her favorite son away, weeping bitterly. What had she done? What good was her life if Jacob chose the wrong woman for his wife? She took comfort when Isaac charged Jacob to pass by the daughters of Canaan, go to Rebekah's father, and take a wife from among the daughters of Laban, her brother. Yet again and again she remembered the bitter enmity she had sown between her sons because of her terrible desire for Jacob to rule.

JACOB

GENESIS 25:19–49:33

Jacob came into the world clutching his twin brother's heel. This was symbolic of struggles to come. Jacob contended with his older brother Esau over the birthright and the blessing of their father, Isaac. Jacob won, but only through deception. The story of the enmity and eventual reconciliation of these patriarchs is told later in this book in the account of Esau.

After stealing the blessing from Esau, Jacob fled to northern Syria to live with his uncle Laban. During the journey he stopped one night to sleep and used a rock for a pillow. There Jacob had a dream of a ladder that reached from earth to heaven. Angels were climbing up and down on this ladder. In the dream, the Lord promised Jacob that his descendants would cover the earth and that He would be with Jacob in his travels.

When he awoke Jacob was frightened and said, "This is the house of God and the gate of heaven!" He named the place Bethel and promised that if God would take care of him, he would always worship God and return to the Lord a tenth of everything he ever received.

Welcomed into his uncle Laban's household, Jacob fell in love with Laban's daughter Rachel. He told Laban he would work for him seven years if Laban would give him Rachel's hand in marriage. Laban agreed.

The seven years flew by, or so it seemed to Jacob. He was head over heels in love with Rachel. When Laban arranged the wedding, he gave his older daughter Leah to be Jacob's wife instead of Rachel. Jacob furiously protested. Laban explained the custom—the oldest daughter marries first! He promised to let Jacob marry Rachel, too, but only if Jacob would work another seven years! Jacob agreed and eventually had both daughters as wives. But he always preferred Rachel.

God saw that Leah was unloved and allowed her to have children while Rachel was unable to conceive. Jacob had six sons by Leah, two other sons by Leah's maid, and two sons by Rachel's maid. Finally God remembered Rachel and let her have a son of her own; his name was Joseph. Later Rachel died giving birth to her second son—Jacob's twelfth—who was called Benjamin.

In time, relations between Jacob and Laban became very strained. Laban was not happy that Jacob's livestock multiplied and grew healthier than the other herds. Jacob yearned to return with his household to his homeland, but Laban realized that the Lord's blessings on Jacob over the years had had a positive effect on his own fortunes. Ultimately Jacob and his family fled in secret. Laban and his men chased and caught them, but conflict was averted and Jacob and Laban made a pact and parted peacefully.

During the journey back to his homeland, Jacob wrestled with God who appeared in the form of a man. All night they wrestled, and Jacob's hip was thrown out of joint in the struggle, but he was not defeated. As daylight approached and the man began to leave, Jacob refused to let Him go until he received a blessing from the divine opponent.

"From now on," the man said, "your name will be Israel, because you have wrestled with God and with men and have won."

ESAU

GENESIS 25:21–34; 26:34–35; 27:1–28:9;
32:3–21; 33:1–16; 36:1–19

E sau and Jacob were twin brothers, sons of Isaac and Rebekah. Their relationship was not a peaceful one. Even inside their mother's womb they clashed. "Two nations are inside your womb," God explained to Rebekah. "One will be stronger, and the older will serve the younger." Esau was delivered first, with Jacob following behind clutching his brother's heel. And, as God had said, Esau was left out of the Hebrew lineage despite his birthright as the firstborn son.

It happened this way: Isaac came to favor Esau as the boy grew because Esau was an excellent hunter and brought his father wild game to eat. Jacob, more inclined toward domestic life, became Rebekah's favorite. One day Esau came home from the wilds extremely hungry and asked for some of the stew Jacob was cooking. "Trade me your birthright for it," Jacob said. Famished, Esau unthinkingly swore to give Jacob his birthright.

Some time later this verbal theft of Esau's birthright came into effect when Rebekah and Jacob tricked Isaac, who was old and blind, into granting his blessing to Jacob. Isaac had sent Esau into the wild to kill an animal and prepare the meat in Isaac's favorite way. Isaac promised that after he ate the wild game he would bless Esau. Rebekah overheard Isaac's words and told Jacob to kill some goats nearby. She used them to prepare the special meal and sent Jacob into Isaac's tent dressed in Esau's clothes and the skins of the goats so he would smell and feel like Esau. Isaac would never know the difference. Jacob served his father the meal and received the blessing of the firstborn son in place of Esau.

The ruse worked. Jacob received the blessing that by right should have been given to Esau, the true firstborn. Part of the blessing was the headship of the family. "May all who curse you be cursed, and all who bless you be blessed," Isaac said.

Shortly afterward Esau returned with the game, prepared it the way his father liked, and took it to Isaac hoping to receive his blessing. But Isaac could not revoke the blessing he had already given Jacob even though he had made a mistake. So Esau was designated to serve his younger brother just as God had foretold. Esau was furious and vowed to kill Jacob as soon as their father died. So Jacob fled to Haran to live with their uncle Laban.

Many years later, Jacob sought to reconcile with Esau. Imagine Jacob's fear when Esau came to meet him with an army of several hundred men! Jacob sent a generous offering of livestock to Esau. As they approached each other, Jacob bowed low seven times to pay homage to his brother. Esau forgot his wrath and tearfully ran to embrace and forgive Jacob for his deception.

Pardon can rarely be as moving as when Esau reconciled with the brother who had stolen his birthright.

RACHEL

GENESIS 29–31, 35

Of the many tasks necessary to keep her father's household and holdings running smoothly, his younger daughter Rachel best liked caring for the sheep. Sometimes her older sister Leah chided her about it. "Why can't you be like other women, instead of always wanting to be off with a smelly bunch of animals?" She pulled a long face. "You won't see me chasing after unruly lambs or rams and ewes that have to be pulled from thickets." Leah delicately pinched her nostrils with a thumb and forefinger. "No man will seek your hand when you smell like dirty, wet wool."

Rachel only laughed. What cared she? Still young in years, she had plenty of time to find a husband. She refrained from saying so. For some reason, Leah had waited year after year for love to seek her out but remained unbetrothed. Rachel loved her sister and could not understand why men passed Leah by. Perhaps if she hadn't been so busy tending sheep, Rachel would have spent more time peering into a pool of water, noticing the reflection of a beautiful, well-favored young woman—whose charms made Leah's tender eyes pale into insignificance by comparison.

One day Rachel and her flocks came to a well in the field, as was her custom. A great stone lay rolled in the well's mouth. When all the flocks of sheep were gathered, the stone was rolled away and the shepherds watered the sheep. This day a strange young man stood nearby. Rachel hesitated, feeling hot color steal into her smooth cheeks and not knowing why.

To her surprise, he came straight to her. "You are the daughter of Laban, son of Nahor?"

"Why—yes. I am Rachel." Her heart pounded.

"I have traveled far. I am your kinsman Jacob, son of Isaac who married Rebekah, sister of Laban." He kissed Rachel, lifted up his voice, and wept.

Rachel broke free, stared, then ran to tell her father. More than the exertion of running made her heart beat more wildly than ever. That unruly member continued to leap in the most unmaidenly way all through the month Jacob abode with Laban and his family. Rachel hid it as best she could and refused to even discuss Jacob with Leah.

At the end of the month, Jacob struck a bargain with Laban. "Rachel has found favor in my sight. I will serve thee seven years for her hand."

Laban saw the chance to gain an expert workman. "It is better that I give her to thee, than to another man: Abide with me."

For seven years, Jacob served Laban, never suspecting the scheme in the other's cunning mind. When the marriage feast finally came, Laban exchanged Leah for Rachel! The next day, Jacob bitterly accused him of treachery. Laban replied that in their country the firstborn must wed before the younger. "You shall also have Rachel if you vow to serve seven more years," he promised.

Rachel, who had been distraught at her sister's marriage to Jacob, felt hope stir in her heart. Yet it seemed much to ask. Fourteen years, for the love of a maiden? Such a thing had never before been done in her country.

"I will serve," Jacob huskily told Laban, gaze steady on Rachel. Nothing could have showed Rachel better how much she was loved—far more than her sister Leah ever could be. It sustained her through the years when Leah bore strong sons and a daughter, but Rachel remained barren.

But God had not forgotten Rachel. Finally, she conceived and bore a son. She praised the Lord, crying, "God hath taken away my reproach." She called her son Joseph, meaning "he shall add." She also said, "The Lord shall add to me another son," and kept the foreknowledge close in her heart.

Rachel died birthing Benjamin, her second son, and was buried on the way to Bethlehem. Her name lives on as a mother in Israel who loved her husband, her children, and her God.

LEAH

L eah, daughter of Laban, hated the elder-sister role life had forced her to play. Why must a woman with a loving heart be condemned to idleness simply because no man had yet spoken for her? Must she forever be compared with another, always unfavorably?

Leah loved Rachel. Sometimes she exulted in the girl's young beauty. More often she despaired. In her deepest soul-searching, she honestly admitted it was unreasonable to believe anyone would pass fair Rachel by in favor of the elder sister. Her lip curled. The few who had did so with an eye to Laban's holdings, not for love of his daughter. She would have none of them.

The day their kinsman Jacob came, Leah felt a stirring deep inside. Here was a man who more than fulfilled her secret dreams. Strong, gentle, his very presence made Leah's heart throb with longing, then grow numb at the look in his eyes. There was no room in his heart for anyone but Rachel.

In spite of the knowledge, Leah refused to accept defeat. Had she not seven years to show herself as worthy as Rachel, if not as beautiful? Even when months fled into years and the marriage feast day drew near, a slim hope remained. Would Laban, powerful as he was, break tradition and allow his younger daughter to wed first?

In a twinkling, everything changed. Leah could scarcely grasp the rapid change in her life. She, not Rachel, became Jacob's wife. Triumph blotted out all else—until the next morning. Hope of his loving her vanished when Jacob discovered Laban's deceit. Leah wondered if she would ever forget the sight of his face when he beheld her, not Rachel, for whom he had toiled so long. Like a slim, keen blade, it plunged into her heart, twisting and turning when her father extracted Jacob's vow to serve another seven years in exchange for Rachel. Now she lay sleepless, passionately wishing her husband lay by her side and not her sister's. She could imagine them whispering, perhaps blaming her as well as Laban. At times she writhed, wishing she had never seen the man who became her husband, then passionately clutching at the shreds of his love with both hands in an attempt to convince herself one day he would care.

When the Lord saw Leah was not loved, He blessed her with children. With each, she felt Jacob must surely learn to love her, especially when her sister remained barren. Instead, Jacob's heart lingered with Rachel, his first and only real love. Six strong sons and one beautiful daughter Leah gave her husband, rejoicing in each, clinging to the fading vision of one day possessing Jacob's heart.

After the birth of Dinah, God hearkened unto Rachel and she conceived. Jacob's countenance wore joy far beyond any he had ever shown over the arrival of a child by Leah. Again hurt flayed his first wife.

Leah faced greater conflict once Rachel delivered her son Benjamin. Jacob, now called Israel, could not hide the fact he cared far more for Joseph and Benjamin, Rachel's sons, than his other sons and daughter.

Though she desperately tried, Leah never recaptured the brief triumph she had known on her marriage day. As in girlhood, her fair young sister's shadow lay over Leah all the days of her life.

Joseph, the Son of Jacob

Genesis 37, 39–50

Was he arrogant or just sincerely proud? Whichever, Joseph grated on the nerves of his ten older brothers. He clearly was their father's favorite. Jacob had even given him a special gift of a lavishly colored coat.

Not only so, Joseph had the audacity to tell his brothers about his dreams—stories of symbolic bundles of wheat and celestial bodies which implied that the brothers would some day pay Joseph homage.

One day as Joseph's brothers tended sheep, they saw the boy coming across the field. "Here comes that dreamer," they scoffed and conspired to put an end to Joseph's insolence. They would have killed him but for the mercy of Reuben, their oldest sibling. He proposed they throw him into a dry well. This they did. But when a caravan of Ishmaelites en route to Egypt happened by, they sold Joseph to them as a slave. Thus the lineage of Abraham was diverted to this foreign land.

Although only a slave, Joseph prospered in Egypt. His master, Potiphar, the commander of Pharaoh's palace guard, placed Joseph in charge of his entire household. But this favored position was not to last. Potiphar's wife, impressed by the handsome young man, tried to seduce Joseph. When he refused, she connived to have him jailed.

But still the Lord brought Joseph back to prominence, this time through his timely interpretation of Pharaoh's troubling dreams. Joseph told Pharaoh that his dreams indicated there would soon be seven years of abundant crops in Egypt followed by seven years of famine. Pharaoh heeded this warning and stored up reserves of grain for the coming hard times and made Joseph the governor of the whole country—even though he was still a slave!

A dramatic family reunion came when, during the famine,

Joseph's brothers journeyed to Egypt to buy food. Of course, they did not recognize Joseph, and he played a hard game with them. The youngest brother, Benjamin, who was Jacob's favorite, was set up as a thief. This warranted severe punishment in Egypt. But Judah, one of the older brothers, assumed the blame for Benjamin. Joseph was so moved by this that he revealed his identity and tearfully welcomed them. And the brothers paid him homage just as the dreams had said. Jacob's entire household relocated to Egypt during this difficult time, and Joseph took care of them.

In time, however, the descendants of Jacob would become slaves of the Egyptians because no one like Joseph remained in power to look after their interests. This set the stage for the dramatic Exodus of the children of Israel and their odyssey to the Promised Land.

POTIPHAR'S WIFE

GENESIS 39

Potiphar's wife eyed the well-favored young slave her Egyptian husband had acquired some time before. A slow smile crept over her painted lips. What an open-faced youngster this Joseph was! Her sluggish blood, jaded by many conquests, stirred. Young men always attracted her. She licked her lips like a giant cat savoring its prey long before securing it.

"Where did you find him?" she asked.

Potiphar, captain of the guard and highly respected, smiled at her. No one dared inform him of his wife's indiscretions. To do so meant risking terrible punishment. Even if one spoke, Potiphar would not believe. His fierce, possessive love blinded him to the wickedness thinly veiled to all but him.

"An interesting story." He glanced at Joseph and paused. The woman reclining on a couch saw a flicker of pain in the young slave's face. "You may go," Potiphar told Joseph, who gracefully walked away. It brought another gleam to the wife's eyes.

"He seems—healthy."

"He's far more than that. He has served so well I have put him in charge of all my affairs. Never have I had such an overseer." A strange look crossed Potiphar's face. "Since he took charge, my holdings have increased." He laughed. "Joseph says his God has blessed this house and my fields."

"His god!" A quick swing of her feet brought the woman to a sitting position. "Which one? Osiris, god of the underworld?"

Potiphar shook his head. "No. Joseph worships one he calls Jehovah. He says there are no other gods. Anyway, the boy was born to his father's favorite wife in later years. The old man loved Joseph more than his half-brothers and made him a coat of many colors. It made the others hate him. Things worsened when Joseph told of a dream that when interpreted meant he would rule over his family and they would one day bow down to him."

"I should think it would!" Interest whetted, Potiphar's wife disdainfully flicked a hand. If she chose to pursue her interest in the young man, he needn't think she would bow to him—or any other.

"Most of the brothers wanted to kill him, but Reuben, the eldest, intervened. He convinced them to shed no blood but cast the boy into a pit. Later they sold him to a band of Ishmaelites who brought him to Egypt. A good day for us," he added.

"A good day," she agreed, her fingers stroking her silken draperies.

Potiphar's wife bided her time, taking care to act circumspectly in front of her husband but casting meaningful glances toward Joseph on every possible occasion. He seemed not to see them. It baffled her. Was he so innocent he could not see her invitation? Or so clever he chose to ignore it? The thought sent scarlet flags to her cheeks.

One day when Potiphar was not home, his wife summoned Joseph and sent away her maids. Her heart raced with excitement. "Come." She gestured to the couch where she lay.

Joseph refused, saying he could sin neither against his master nor his God.

Potiphar's wife hid her rage and shrugged. He would lay aside his scruples soon enough. Yet time after time, Joseph continued to refuse her advances. His reluctance goaded her on until she determined to break his will.

One afternoon when no other men were in the house, Joseph once more turned down her invitation. She snatched his garment. He fled, leaving it in her hand. Enraged at being rejected, she cried in a loud voice, "See? The Hebrew came in to mock me. When I cried out, he fled, leaving his garment." She told the same tale to her husband when he came home. None of the household dared deny her lies.

Potiphar's wrath was kindled against the young man he had trusted with all he possessed. He comforted his sobbing wife and had Joseph thrown into prison. He never knew his wife rejoiced—then decked herself out for her next conquest.

MOSES

EXODUS, LEVITICUS, NUMBERS,
AND DEUTERONOMY

He was born in the worst of times. Not only were his people, the Hebrews, slaves in Egypt; the pharaoh had decreed that because the slaves were multiplying so fast, every newborn Hebrew boy must be drowned in the Nile. Therefore, Moses' mother kept him hidden for the first three months of his life. When she could keep him no longer, she set him adrift in a reed basket along the edge of the Nile River. The basket was discovered by Pharaoh's daughter. After Moses' own mother raised him, he was adopted into the royal family.

One day, the young man Moses saw an Egyptian beating a Hebrew slave. Moses rushed to his kinsman's defense and killed the Egyptian. Fearing he would be reported and executed, Moses buried the Egyptian in the sand and fled to the land of Midian. There he married and settled down to work as a shepherd. But God had a very important task in mind for Moses. God's people, the Hebrews, were slaves in Egypt and desperately needed a leader to confront Pharaoh and demand their release.

Moses was quietly tending his father-in-law's livestock on Mount Horeb one day when God appeared to him in a burning bush. God commanded the exile to return to Egypt and lead the Hebrews to freedom.

Moses protested, "Who am I to do this?"

"I will be with you," the Lord replied and commissioned Moses to go in the name of the great "I Am." Then Moses complained that he was not a good orator. So God agreed to let Aaron, Moses' older brother, be his spokesman. God spoke to Moses, and Moses relayed God's messages through Aaron.

Moses and Aaron appeared boldly before Pharaoh. The Lord punished Pharaoh's stubbornness by singular means, and the Hebrews ultimately escaped under the leadership of Moses. The Red

Sea waters opened, and the people were free. This story is an unparalleled epic. Of equal impact is its sequel: The freed masses were mutinous and contentious. Even Moses' own brother Aaron and his sister Miriam joined in their antics. As this horde wandered toward the Promised Land, God, through Moses, gave them the Ten Commandments and other laws.

Moses was faithful to the Lord. But there was an occasion in the Zin Desert when Moses disobeyed the Lord. This failure bred disrespect for God among the people, so God did not allow Moses to enter Canaan, the land he had promised to Israel. Before Moses died, however, God let him glimpse the land from the top of Mount Nebo across the Jordan River from Canaan. So Moses died in Moab, and his successor Joshua led the Hebrews into Canaan.

AARON

When God commanded Moses to lead the Hebrews out of Egypt, Moses begged to be excused. "I am not an eloquent speaker," he complained. So God allowed Moses to engage his older brother Aaron to be his spokesman. So Aaron transmitted to the people God's words to Moses.

Moses' and Aaron's encounters with Pharoah in which God demanded, "Let My people go," are among the most dramatic portions of Scripture. They provide riveting lessons in divine patience and punishment. God performed astonishing miracles through Moses and Aaron—such as turning a stick into a snake and changing the Nile River into blood. God sent a string of catastrophes upon the Egyptians, which culminated in the historic night when death visited the firstborn son of every Egyptian household. Still Pharoah refused to release Israel or respect their God. Aaron is not always mentioned in the narrative of the Bible, but he was always at Moses' side.

The Exodus of Israel climaxed with their passage through the Red Sea and God's annihilation of the Egyptian army who had stubbornly followed them. Then, years passed when Israel wandered in the wilderness and sorely tried the patience of Moses and Aaron. As leaders, they did as the Lord commanded, but the people repeatedly lost faith. When thirsty or hungry or facing a hostile army, the Hebrews complained bitterly. Yet God met their needs in miraculous ways. One would think the wandering Hebrews, more than any other people in history, would have believed because they repeatedly saw God's power and faithfulness—yet they doubted and rebelled against their leaders.

Aaron was also given a task beyond that of spokesman. God made him the high priest and instructed that he be lavishly and meticulously attired for this position. Only Aaron and his descendants were authorized to offer sacrifices for the Israelites. Yet even Aaron lost faith. On one occasion, when Moses was alone on Mount Sinai for an extended period with the Lord, the people became restless and persuaded Aaron to make for them the image of a god. So Aaron melted gold into a calf-shaped idol for the people to worship. They believed it was the god that had brought them out of Egypt!

This misplaced allegiance and loss of control led to bloodshed, and Moses had to intercede before the Lord on behalf of the people. In response, God forgave them and promised to remain with Israel. But because of Aaron's flawed leadership and the people's diminished respect for God as a result, God did not allow Aaron to enter the Promised Land.

When the time came for Aaron to die, the Lord instructed Moses to go with his brother to the top of Mount Hor. There Moses removed Aaron's beautiful robe and placed it on Aaron's son Eleazar, thus designating him as the next high priest. Aaron died and the Israelites spent thirty days in mourning for their leader and high priest.

MOSES' MOTHER

EXODUS 2

Strange thoughts troubled the king of Egypt. He was new to the throne, and his perplexities rose daily. Some he could shunt off to his advisors but not the ever growing problem he encountered each time he gazed on his subjects. The children of Israel who dwelt in the land were fruitful. They increased abundantly. They multiplied and waxed exceedingly mighty until the land was filled with them. He abominated them all and, worse, feared what they might become and do.

The king said to his people, "Behold, the people of the children of Israel are more and mightier than we. We must deal wisely with them. If war should come they would join our enemies and fight against us, and so get them up out of the land." The corners of his mouth drew down, and he swished his royal robes.

At the king's orders, taskmasters were appointed to afflict the children of Israel with their burdens. They were held in bitter bondage and forced to build for Pharaoh treasure cities, Pithom and Raamses. In mortar and brick and all manner of service of the fields they were made to serve, to endure the hardship or drop and be beaten. Death offered the only freedom. For four hundred years, they were enslaved. Yet the more the Egyptians afflicted them, the more the Israelites multiplied and grew.

Could nothing stop them? The king ordered the Hebrew midwives to perform a terrible task. At the time of delivery, daughters might live; every son must be killed. The midwives feared God. They saved the men children alive, in spite of their orders to the contrary.

The king called for them and demanded, "Why have ye done this thing?"

The midwives said unto Pharaoh, "The Hebrew women are lively, not like the Egyptian women. They are delivered ere we come in unto them." God dealt well with the midwives, and the people continued to multiply and wax mighty.

Determined not to be outwitted, Pharaoh charged all his people, saying, "Every son that is born ye shall cast into the river, and every daughter ye shall save alive." A wailing in Egypt rose that assaulted the ears of its inhabitants as the dark river waters swallowed up countless innocent male children.

About this time, a daughter of the house of Levi, married to Amram, also of the house of Levi, conceived. Jochebed bore a son. She refused to comply with the king's edict, believing somehow the child must be saved. For three terrifying months she concealed her child, but the time came when she could no longer keep him without discovery.

"I cannot let my baby be destroyed," she whispered into the shawl that held him. A plan born of desperation formed. She made an ark of bulrushes, a floating basket daubed with slime and pitch to keep the water out. Jochebed carefully tucked the child in its depths, covered him, and eased it in the flags by the brink of the river that had claimed the lives of so many other babies.

Why must such things be? her aching heart silently cried. *Then, Lord God of Israel, protect my little son.*

"Stay hidden by the river," Jochebed commanded her daughter Miriam. "Watch the ark carefully. We must know what happens to this, thy brother." She stumbled away, knowing she had done all she could to save her child but wondering how she could stand the pain.

Some time later, her daughter Miriam rushed home. "Mother, mother!" Her childish, treble voice rose to a high, excited pitch. "Pharaoh's daughter found the ark." She stopped for breath. "You are to nurse the baby—for wages!"

Never in her wildest imaginations had Jochebed envisioned such an outcome. The best she had hoped was for a kindly soul to rescue the child and conceal it as she could no longer do. Jochebed fell to her knees. "Blessed be the Lord God of Israel," she cried. "Jehovah has heard my prayer and this day delivered my son by His mighty hand." A little later, she settled down, nursing the son doomed to die by Pharaoh's decree but spared by God for a mighty, world-changing role.

MOSES' SISTER

EXODUS 2, 15; NUMBERS 12

Small Miriam carefully held the tiny bundle her mother had placed in her eager arms. Eyes round, she touched the miniature fingers and gently stroked the baby's soft cheek. "Mother, he is so beautiful. Surely God will not allow him to die." She hopefully looked up at Jochebed, busy with bulrushes, slime, and pitch.

Her mother sighed. "I hope not, child. Yet other beautiful children have died by order of the wicked pharaoh. If only we could leave this land of bondage! How long, oh, Lord, how long?"

The familiar cry for freedom, kept low to keep from disturbing the sleeping baby, rang loud in Miriam's ears. Child that she was, she yet recognized the longing. It echoed in her heart. "If we are Jehovah's chosen people, why does He allow us to be oppressed?" she fiercely demanded.

"Hush, Miriam. It is not for us to question the ways of Jehovah. Besides—" Jochebed's nimble fingers stilled, and a faraway look came to her eyes. She lowered her voice to a whisper, and her daughter leaned closer. Even walls had ears these days. No one knew how idle words crept into the wind, but speaking of certain subjects meant harsh punishments, even death.

"My child, one day a deliverer will be sent, one to lead God's people out of this land and into a place of freedom."

A deliverer. In a passion she could not describe, Miriam fiercely whispered, "When will the deliverer come?" Her gaze dropped to the little brother she loved with all the feelings of her young heart. "Mother, why does Jehovah not send the deliverer now, when we need him so badly?"

"We cannot know the ways of the Lord," Jochebed sadly told her. She continued smearing the ark with slime and pitch. "There, it is finished. When it dries, it will be the finest small boat anyone could ask. We shall pray for it to safely carry your brother to someone who will care for him."

A little later, Miriam watched her mother place the baby in his new floating cradle. Awake now, he made no cry. Jochebed laid the ark on the water, admonished her daughter to keep watch, and trudged away.

For a time nothing happened. Then a rustle warned Miriam someone approached. She made herself small in her hiding place.

"Why, what is that?" someone said.

Miriam gasped and peeked from shelter. The pharaoh's daughter stood a short distance away. Her maid drew the basket with the baby from the water. The compassion in the look Pharaoh's daughter bestowed on the crying baby gave Miriam courage to spring forth and ask if she should bring a Hebrew nurse for the child. On winged, bare feet, she sped to her mother with the gladsome news.

Miriam became a fine woman, respected by her people. She served as a prophetess, skilled with timbrel and dancing, singing praises to the Lord, and rejoicing over the goodness of God. Yet in spite of her calling, she at one time allowed jealousy to influence her and spoke against Moses for marrying an Ethiopian woman. "Hath the Lord spoken only by Moses?" she and Aaron demanded. "Hath he not also spoken by us?"

A strangled cry arose from Moses and Aaron.

They speechlessly pointed.

Miriam looked down at her hands and tottered. Her skin had turned white as snow from leprosy. "Oh, God, what have I done?" she wailed.

Moses cried to the Lord on her behalf, imploring Him to remove the curse. The Lord in his goodness hearkened unto Moses' pleadings, but for seven long days Miriam was shut out of the camp for her rebelliousness. After she rejoined the others, she again became respected and never tired of telling how Jehovah saved Moses, the deliverer who freed the Israelite people from Pharaoh's cruel hand and led them to the Promised Land.

PHARAOH'S DAUGHTER

EXODUS 2

In the eyes of those who dwelt in Egypt, Pharaoh's daughter had everything a girl or woman could desire. The finest silks and cloth of gold clothed her. Jewels lay unworn in costly caskets, simply because of their number. The very stars in the heavens could not outshine Pharaoh's daughter when her maidens decked her out.

Only one thing she did not have: peace of mind. Naturally compassionate and kindhearted, she raged when her father the king ordered the Hebrew midwives Shiphrah and Puah to kill all sons of the Hebrew children when they were called to serve in their office. She secretly rejoiced when the midwives did not obey the commandment. How clever of them to say the Hebrew women were more lively than those of Egypt and had already delivered the children by the time the midwives came!

One day the daughter of Pharaoh went to the special place in the river where she washed herself. She walked along the river's side, anticipating the clean, fresh coolness awaiting in the secluded spot she had made her own. Yet today a foreign presence had entered her domain. Something rocked among the flags.

"Bring it to me that I might behold it," Pharaoh's daughter ordered her maid. The servant obeyed. Pharaoh's daughter bent low over the retrieved object. "Why, it's an ark, fashioned of bulrushes, daubed with slime and pitch! How came such a thing to my bathing place?"

Nimble fingers opened the ark. Pharaoh's daughter's eyes grew wide at sight of the contents. A tiny wail issued from the basket. Fear clutched the girl's heart. She sent a hasty glance back toward her maidens. "Be gone! I will remain here for a time."

Giggling and fluttering, they hastened to obey. When only her maid remained, Pharaoh's daughter drew forth the babe. Compassion filled her soul. "This is one of the Hebrews' children." Color fled from her face. "What shall we do? If father knows the small one lives, he will order the babe thrown into the river, as so many before him. His life will be snuffed out like a candle in the wind." She held the tiny boy close to her beating heart, and he nestled against her. "It shall not be! He is mine."

A small voice beside her whispered, "Shall I go and call to thee a nurse of the Hebrew women, that she may nurse the child for thee?"

Pharaoh's daughter whirled, the babe still clutched close to her bosom. Liquid brown eyes stared out of a smooth face. Something in their depths silently assured Pharaoh's daughter she had nothing to fear from the Hebrew girl-child before her. "Go," she commanded.

With fast beating heart, she waited the short time that felt like hours. The Hebrew child returned, holding an older woman by the hand. The suffering of the Israelite people shone in the woman's eyes, but her gaze met Pharaoh's daughter honestly. Again came a feeling of trust. "Take this child away and nurse it for me, and I will give thee wages," Pharaoh's daughter ordered. She noted the way the woman's gentle hands accepted the wrapped babe, the instinctive cuddling that came only from a woman who possessed great love for all children.

"His name is Moses," Pharaoh's daughter said. "For I drew him from the water. He shall be my son."

Level gaze met level gaze. The woman smiled and bowed. A strange, mystical expression crept into her eyes. "It is well." She bowed again and walked away with her charge.

Pharaoh's daughter stared after her, wondering. The Hebrew nurse's face had filled with such radiance that in spite of her rude clothing, she appeared lovelier by far than the pharaoh's daughter in all her glory.

ZIPPORAH

EXODUS 2, 18

Reuel, the priest of Midian (also called Jethro) had seven daughters. Zipporah, "the bird," was one of them. A maiden's life in the land of Midian was not easy. Time after time when the girls came to the well to draw water, fill the troughs, and water their father's flocks, unfriendly shepherds drove them away, mocking, laughing, and calling out crude jests. Even Zipporah, strong and unafraid, could not stand against them. They were forced to wait long before watering the sheep.

One day Reuel's daughters came home to their father, driving their flocks and arriving far earlier than was their custom.

"How is it that ye are come so soon today?" he inquired.

A babble of voices arose, excited and incoherent.

"Silence!" their father commanded. "Speak one at a time so a man can comprehend what it is you wish to convey."

His daughters obeyed, but eyes and faces shone with the startling occurrence that had taken place earlier in the day.

"We took the flock to the well for water," one began.

"The shepherds came as usual to drive us away," another said.

"Suddenly an Egyptian came, we know not from whence." The story grew even more amazing. "He dealt hardly with the shepherds and delivered us out of their hands."

"That isn't all," several chorused. One added, "The stranger also drew water enough for us and watered the flock that we might not have it to do."

Reuel marveled and said unto his daughters, "Where is he? why is it that ye have left the man? call him, that he may eat bread."

Weary from his long journey, sick at heart over having slain an Egyptian he found smiting his Israelite brethren, Moses gladly accepted the kindly priest's offer of shelter and sustenance. He had left Egypt after a Hebrew who strove with another asked, "Who made thee a judge over us? intendest thou to kill me, as thou killedst the Egyptian?" At that moment, Moses realized his deed was known, and he was in great danger from Pharaoh. Here in Midian he could abide in safety.

Zipporah looked on Moses with favor. Unlike the men of her own country, his deep gaze sent warmth to her skin and longing to her heart. The day her father gave her to be Moses' wife brought joy beyond belief. So did the birth of their son. Moses insisted the child be called Gershom and said, "I have been a stranger in a strange land."

Zipporah tried hard to understand the things her husband told her. Still she wondered. What manner of man saw burning bushes that were not consumed? And talked with Jehovah, as a man to a friend?

Greater questions were yet to come, then a long separation. After traveling with her husband to Egypt, where his brethren were enslaved, Zipporah's heart ached when Moses sent her back to her father in Midian to wait there with their sons Gershom and Eliezer. Tales came to them of the many plagues visited on the Egyptians because of the hardness of Pharaoh's heart and the release of the Israelites after the death of the Egyptians' firstborn. More stories rode the wind: the parting of a sea to provide dry land on which Moses and his followers trod. The rush of water once they were safe that drowned the attacking Egyptian army. The children of Israel, fed manna in the wilderness.

At times Zipporah wondered if she would ever again cast her gaze on the man who captured her love but held true to a higher calling. At last, great happiness came. Jethro heard of what God had done for Moses. He took Zipporah, Gershom, and Eliezer and came to the tents of Moses in the wilderness. Jethro rejoiced for the goodness the Lord had done and said, "Now I know the Lord is greater than all gods: For in the thing wherein they dealt proudly He was above them." Zipporah's joy knew no bounds—and she marveled at what a mighty leader her husband Moses had become.

BALAAM

NUMBERS 22:5–24:25

God's sacred book, the Bible, occasionally contains true humor ranging from Old Testament foibles to the exaggerated illustrations used by Christ Himself. (Envision a camel passing through the eye of a needle!)

Here is Balaam, a soothsayer from Mesopotamia, riding his donkey to visit King Balak of Moab. King Balak has a problem: The Israelites, wandering from Egypt to the Promised Land have arrived at the Jordan River, and Balak sees them as a threat to his kingdom. They are God's chosen people and have already conquered entire armies. Balak does not want to fight them; he knows the Israelites are too strong. Yet if they remain in his territory, Balak fears they will consume everything in sight. They must be driven away.

Balak has a solution: Summon Balaam and have this Gentile prophet place a curse on the Israelites. He does so and promises Balaam a handsome reward.

Balaam wrestles with this proposal. When the Lord tells him plainly that the Israelites have God's own blessing, Balaam dutifully refuses Balak's request. "How can I curse what the Lord has blessed?" he reasons. Balak persists, and God permits Balaam to go to the king. "But do only what I tell you to do," the Lord commands. The Lord wants to impress upon Balaam his unhappiness with Balak's proposal and the importance of Balaam's strict obedience in this situation. The fact that God chooses to do this is memorable.

On the way to Moab, Balaam receives a sequence of rude surprises by his donkey. First the animal suddenly leaves the road and carries him into a field. Later, the donkey brushes against a stone wall, scraping Balaam's foot. Then the donkey lies down and refuses to move. Each time, Balaam angrily beats the poor creature. What Balaam has failed to see is that on each occasion, the donkey has been halted by an angel with a sword. Finally, Balaam gets the greatest surprise of all: The donkey looks at him and speaks!

"Why are you beating me?" asks the donkey.

"Because you embarrassed me," rebukes the astonished rider. "If I had a sword, I would kill you."

"Have I ever acted this way before?" challenges the donkey.

Upon reflection, Balaam has to admit, "No."

While the distracted diviner is discoursing with his donkey in what is perhaps the most hilarious scene in the entire Bible, the Lord reveals the angel to him. The awestruck traveler bows to his knees, apologizes for beating his frightened donkey, and offers to return home, if God so desires. The angel instructs Balaam to proceed to Moab but reminds him to say exactly what the Lord tells him to say.

Balaam follows God's bidding and instead of cursing the Israelites, he blesses them three times, to King Balak's chagrin. The king sends Balaam away, thinking him a fool for squandering the chance to earn a king's reward. But Balaam corrects him: "Even if you offered me a house full of money, I could not disobey the Lord." These are bold words to say to an angry king! But in the wake of his experience with the donkey, Balaam understood very clearly who was the true King.

JOSHUA

DEUTERONOMY 31:1–8; 34:5–9; JOSHUA

Y ou're the one who will lead our people into God's Promised Land."

Those words, spoken by the aging Moses, must have thrilled Joshua's heart—and given him much trepidation. There were strong nations to conquer once the Hebrews crossed the Jordan River. "Do not be afraid," Moses told him. "God Himself will lead you. He will not abandon you."

Israel reached the Jordan near Jericho at flood time. A crossing seemed impossible. But God told Joshua He would perform a miracle to display the fact that God's blessings were with him. And sure enough, when the priests carrying the ark of God's covenant waded into the swollen waters, the river stopped flowing! The people were able to go across the dry river bottom.

One day near Jericho, Joshua encountered an angel with a sword. "Are you friend or foe?" Joshua asked, thinking the angel was human.

"Neither," the angel replied. "I am captain of the Lord's army."

Joshua bowed low to the angel, who commanded him to take off his sandals. "You're standing on holy ground," the angel said.

Joshua may be remembered best for the capture of Jericho. It was a well-guarded city, but the Lord told Joshua it was his for the taking. God's tactic was simple but strange. The Israelite army, led by priests carrying the ark of the covenant, was to march around the city for six days. On the seventh day, the priests were to blow trumpets while soldiers marched around the city seven times. Then as the trumpets sounded one extended note, the soldiers were to shout, and the walls of Jericho would collapse!

In this way Jericho was leveled and its inhabitants annihilated. Joshua placed the Lord's curse on anyone who might try to rebuild the city.

At long last the Israelites settled in Canaan, the Promised Land.

Joshua ruled wisely, and the Lord sent miracles to help Joshua's army subdue their enemies. Joshua divided the land among the Israelites and renewed their covenant with the Lord. He gave his people a choice: Worship the one true God and be blessed, or keep worthless idols and suffer punishment. "As for my household," said Joshua, "we will serve the Lord."

RAHAB

JOSHUA 2, 6

R ahab, harlot and innkeeper, stared into the faces of the two
strangers who had taken lodging in her house. What manner
of men were they, these bold Israelites who dared enter Jericho?
As she spoke with them, the tittle-tattle that had raced through the
streets of Jericho and into every house kept time with their story. A
strange and unexplainable feeling came, an assurance that all she
had heard of the protecting hand of the Lord who watched over His
chosen people was true. Yet what had she to do with the matter?
The men had obviously come to spy out the land, with full intentions of making it their own. Even now, one of the king's soldiers
would be seeking the Israelites.

Rahab scarcely believed her own ears when she whispered,
"Come!" Heart beating wildly, she led them to the roof of the house.
She hid them under stalks of flax, laid in order on the roof. "Do not
make a sound or you will surely be discovered," she ordered them.
"If you are, you not only bring death to yourselves, but to all of the
house of Rahab." She slipped away.

A loud pounding on the door sent blood hurrying through her
veins. She flung it open. "What want you?" she demanded of the
king's guard.

"In the name of the king, bring forth the men that are come to
thee," came the reply. "It has been told to the king of Jericho they
are children of Israel, come to search out the country."

Rahab didn't betray herself by even the blink of an eyelash.
"There came men to me, but I wist not whence they were; it came
to pass that the men went out, about the time of the shutting of the
gate when darkness fell. Pursue them quickly; for ye shall overtake them."

The king's men eyed her suspiciously; Rahab's steady glance
did not waver. She stood in the doorway until certain they had
gone, then waited a time to make sure none lurked behind to see

if she spoke the truth.

When all grew still, Rahab went back to the roof. She told the spies, "I know the Lord hath given you the land. Your terror is fallen upon us, and all the inhabitants of the land faint because of you. When we heard how the Lord dried up the water of the Red Sea for you when you came out of Egypt, our hearts did melt, neither did there remain any more courage in any man, because of you: For the Lord your God is God in heaven above, and in earth beneath." She paused, hands clenched and wet with sweat.

"I pray you, swear unto me by the Lord, since I have showed you kindness, that you will also show kindness unto my father's house, and give me a true token. . .save alive my father, and my mother, and my brethren, and my sisters, and all that they have, and deliver our lives from death."

The Israelites exchanged glances. They promised Rahab if she kept silent about the whole business, when the Lord gave them the land, they would deal kindly and truly with her.

Great relief filled her. "Come." She took them to the window and let them down by a cord, for her house was upon the town wall, but not before they bade her bind a line of scarlet thread in the same window and bring her family and all their household inside the inn. Whosoever went outside would die. All who remained inside the house with the scarlet thread would be spared.

Rahab did as commanded. When the walls of Jericho fell before Joshua and his men, only Rahab and those with her in the house did not perish. The two young spies she had saved took her and her kindred to the camp of Israel. Her heart burned within her. One act of kindness had brought mercy for those she loved.

The genealogy of Christ given in Matthew 1 lists Rahab as the mother of Boaz, great-grandfather of King David. If this is she who saved Joshua's men, it seems likely Rahab turned from her wickedness and sought forgiveness from the Lord she recognized as God of heaven and earth.

DEBORAH

JUDGES 4–5

Deborah, prophetess and judge of Israel, dwelt beneath her palm tree between Ramah and Bethel. The children of Israel came to her for judgments in disputes they either could not or would not settle on their own. Sometimes Lapidoth, her husband, felt they taxed his wife beyond measure, yet he took great pride in the wisdom of her decisions. Did not all who knew Deborah love and respect her for the high position to which Jehovah had called her?

Not all of Deborah's troubles came from those she served. The Lord had also burdened her concerning her people. War with Sisera, captain of King Jabin's army, loomed as inevitable. Anticipation of the forthcoming battle lay on Deborah's heart like a heavy stone.

One day she called Barak, son of Abinoam out of Kedeshnaphtali, and demanded, "Has the Lord God of Israel not commanded us to go and draw toward Mount Tabor, taking ten thousand men of the children of Naphtali and Zebulun? Jehovah Himself has promised to draw Sisera with his chariots and multitude to the river Kishon and deliver him into our hand."

Barak, resembling the thunderbolt and lightning for which he had been named, flung his head back. "If you will go with me, I will go. If you will not, then I will not go."

Deborah faced him squarely. A dozen thoughts chased through her active brain. A woman in battle, leading against the foe? Such a thing had never been heard of. What would those she judged think of her? *Why not?* she silently asked herself. Had not God called her first as a prophetess, then as a judge? "I will go, notwithstanding the journey you take shall not be for your honor. The Lord shall sell Sisera into the hand of a woman."

Barak agreed and Deborah arose straightway and went with him to Kedesh, where Zebulun and Naphtali awaited them, in answer to Barak's call. Ten thousand men responded and accompanied Barak and Deborah.

On the morning of the battle, Deborah said unto Barak, "Up, for this is the day in which the Lord has delivered Sisera into thine hand."

When Sisera heard that Barak had gone up to Mount Tabor, he gathered together his nine hundred chariots of iron and a multitude of warriors. A terrible battle ensued, but the Lord discomfited Sisera, his chariots, and all his host. When the battle ended, not an enemy remained alive.

Deborah and Barak joined in a song of praise, thanking God for delivering the foes into their hands. They spoke of how God sent a mother in Israel to defeat those who had chosen new gods. They named those who had joined Deborah and Barak in the fray: the princes of Issachar; kings who came and fought without gain of money. They sang, "They fought from heaven; the stars in their courses fought against Sisera."

At last, the ceaseless pounding in Deborah's soul stilled. The land had rest forty years. The name of Deborah took its place in history as one who first judged then led her people both wisely and well.

GIDEON

JUDGES 6–8

He was not a man to be trifled with, as many a foe discovered. Happily, Gideon was on the side of the Israelites.

During the time of the judges God let Israel be subjugated by Midian, and for seven years the children of Israel were impoverished victims of their conquerors.

After they had suffered long enough the Lord spoke to Gideon. This poor Israelite from Ophrah was trying to horde a supply of wheat from his captors, but God had more important work for him to do. God told Gideon, "You will save Israel from the hand of the Midianites."

Gideon was afraid—not only of the assignment, but of his encounter with God. His tribe was weak, Gideon protested, and he was the lowest member of his own family. The Lord responded by bringing the Spirit upon Gideon.

Thus empowered, Gideon sounded a trumpet and sent messengers to gather an army. Thirty-two thousand men initially joined him. "This is too many," God told him. If Israel won the victory with such a large army, the people would assume credit for themselves and deny the power of God. So Gideon invited those who were afraid of fighting to turn back. This left him with ten thousand soldiers.

"Still too many," the Lord said—doubtless stirring Gideon's uneasiness. To reduce the number of soldiers further, God told Gideon to send the soldiers to the water's edge and drink. The ones who lapped the water as a dog would drink were to be separated from those who knelt to drink the water cupped in their hands. Three hundred men lapped to drink. God told Gideon to discharge all the others. "I will deliver the Midianites into your hands."

The Midianites camped in the valley were as thick as locusts; their camels were as numerous as sand on the seashore. Gideon naturally was timid, so the Lord told him to slip into the Midianite camp at night and promised to show him a sign there for reassurance. When Gideon crept near the Midianite camp he heard two men talking. One was relating a dream he'd had of a bread loaf tumbling into camp and flattening one of the tents. His friend interpreted the dream: "The bread loaf is the sword of the Israelite, Gideon. God will deliver the whole Midianite camp into his hands!" Gideon knew his mission was secure.

Gideon and his men took trumpets, jars, and torches and surrounded the Midianite camp. When signaled they sounded the horns, smashed the jars, and waved the torches. The sudden clamor on all sides wakened the Midianites to a scene of total confusion. In their rush to escape, they mistakenly attacked and killed many of their own comrades.

Other Israelites were summoned and completely routed the Midianites. As Gideon and his three hundred commandos chased the Midianite kings across the Jordan River, they wearily stopped at the towns of Succoth and Penuel and requested food, but the leaders of both towns refused to help them. Gideon angrily warned that when he returned with the two kings in tow the insolent town leaders would be punished severely. He was as good as his word. Succoth and Penuel were punished, and the captured kings of Midian were put to death.

The grateful Israelites wanted Gideon and his descendants to be their rulers. But Gideon responded, "The Lord will rule over you."

Gideon's story ends on the unhappy note of forgetfulness and idolatry. In the aftermath of his unprecedented victory, Gideon collected the gold earrings captured from the Midianites. They were melted and cast into an idol, which Gideon took to his hometown of Ophrah. Then, as is the pattern in the book of the Judges, Israel forgot God and gathered in Ophrah to worship Gideon's idol.

SAMSON'S MOTHER

JUDGES 13–15

A certain man named Manoah, whose wife was barren, lived in the midst of the children of Israel, who again did evil in the sight of the Lord and were delivered into the hand of the Philistines for forty years.

One day an angel of the Lord appeared unto the woman and said unto her, "Behold now, thou art barren and bearest not, but thou shalt conceive and bear a son. Now therefore beware, I pray thee, and drink not wine nor strong drink, and eat not any unclean thing: For, lo, thou shalt conceive, and bear a son; and no razor shall come on his head: For the child shall be a Nazarite unto God from the womb: And he shall begin to deliver Israel out of the hand of the Philistines."

Manoah's wife rejoiced greatly and ran to tell her husband. "A man of God came unto me, and his countenance was like the countenance of an angel of God, very terrible: But I asked him not whence he was, neither told he me his name." She faithfully related the rest of the angel's message.

Manoah, much impressed, entreated the Lord, asking for the man of God to come again and teach them what they should do unto the child that would be born. God heard the prayer. The angel came to the woman in the field. She made haste and brought Manoah to him. The angel repeated the instructions he had given earlier but refused to eat bread with them. Manoah took a kid and made an offering. When the flame rose, the angel of the Lord ascended in the flame of the altar. Manoah and his wife looked on it and fell on their faces to the ground.

"We shall surely die," Manoah wailed. "We have seen God."

His wife reminded him God would not have showed them all the things if He planned to kill them. She kept that hope in her heart and one day bore a son. "He shall be called Samson, which means like the sun," she told her husband.

The child grew and the Lord blessed him. When Samson became a young man, a daughter of the Philistines found favor in his eyes. His mother's heart quailed within her. She and Manoah protested, "Is there not a woman among the daughters of thy brethren, or among all our people, that thou goest to take a wife of the uncircumcised Philistines?"

Samson insisted they get her for him, for she pleased him well. Sad-hearted, his mother traveled with her husband and son to the vineyards of Timnath. There a young lion roared against Samson. The Spirit of the Lord came so mightily upon the young man, he killed the lion—but he did not tell his father or mother. Still, they realized their son had been set apart before his birth to do great things.

Samson's mother kept her counsel. The father made a contract with the woman their son desired, and Samson held a great feast. Strong, untamed, uncut hair hanging over his mighty shoulders, he sent a thrill of pride through his mother, although her woman's heart feared for him because he had chosen a Philistine's daughter to wed.

Her fears proved well grounded. Men at the feast threatened to burn the bride and her father's house if she did not entice Samson to give her the answer to a riddle he had posed. If they could declare the answer in the seven days of the feast, they would receive thirty sheets and thirty changes of garments. If not, they would furnish Samson with the same.

The bride wept and teased, saying Samson did not love but hated her. He finally gave her the answer. She immediately told the men of the city. They taunted Samson until his anger kindled and he retaliated, then he went up to his father's house.

Samson's mother grieved for him, even more when he went for his wife and found her father had given her to a companion Samson thought was a friend. Was it for this he had been born? Nay. In spite of doubt, she remembered the angel's words and took comfort: "He shall begin to deliver Israel out of the hand of the Philistines." Perhaps everything that had happened was according to a heavenly plan and a sign that deliverance had started.

SAMSON

JUDGES 13–16

Today's superheroes of sports are weaklings compared to a real hero who lived three thousand years ago. When Samson flexed his muscles, heavy cords snapped like rotten string. He once slew a thousand enemies using the jawbone of an ass for a weapon. He uprooted the gates of the city of Gaza and carried them to the top of a distant hill. When attacked by a lion, he made no attempt to escape or tame the animal; with his bare hands he tore its jaws apart! How many of our professional football stars—or entire championship teams—do you suppose would attempt that?

Samson's feats were the work of the Lord. The Spirit of God came over him, and suddenly he was empowered with incredible strength.

Samson was a Hebrew judge during the years when God allowed the Israelites to fall captive to the Philistines. The wife of the Israelite Manoah learned from an angel of the Lord she would give birth to a son who would rescue the Jews from their captors. When Samson was born, the Holy Spirit came upon him, and he grew to become the Philistines' terror. On one occasion he killed thirty of them. Another time he caught three hundred foxes, tied torches to their tails, and ran them through the Philistines' fields, thus causing their crops to burn. After slaughtering more Philistines, Samson went into the wilderness and lived in a cave.

At one point Samson let himself be captured and turned over to the Philistines. But when his enemies began to celebrate his capture, he snapped his bonds and massacred them.

The Philistines finally found a way to contain him. He fell in love with a woman named Delilah. The Philistine leaders offered her an enormous sum of money if she could find out the source of Samson's strength, as a game. "Tie me up with seven unseasoned bow strings," he told her. "That will normalize my power." Delilah tied him up and summoned the Philistines to come for him. But when he saw them, Samson immediately broke free.

"New ropes will do it," he teased. "Tie me in ropes that have never been used."

Again she tied him, and again he broke his bonds.

Samson had long, wavy hair that had never been cut. "Weave my hair in your loom," he said, "and I'll be as weak as any other man." But again, when Delilah thought she and her conspirators had him at bay, Samson laughingly broke away.

At last he told her the true secret of his strength. "I was dedicated to God when I was born," he said, "so my hair has never been cut. My hair is the key to my strength." Soon Delilah sang him softly to sleep and cut his hair. When he awoke and tried to summon his strength, he found that the Spirit had left him. He was captured. The Philistines put out his eyes, bound him in chains, and threw him in prison where he was forced to grind their grain.

Later the inebriated Philistines were at a festival in honor of their pagan god. They called for Samson to be brought from the dungeon into their temple so they could mock him publicly. Several thousand people were gathered to taunt the once-proud Israelite. But Samson's hair had grown back. He slyly persuaded his guard to position his hands for him between the two main pillars of the temple. Then he prayed that God would strengthen him for one last mighty feat.

God answered his prayer. Samson pushed against the great pillars as hard as he could, they gave way, the temple collapsed on the hordes of Philistine mockers—and on Samson. It is recorded that he killed more Philistines with his last act than he had killed in all his other deeds combined.

DELILAH

JUDGES 16

Delilah of Sorek listened well when the lords of the Philistines came up unto her. Hatred filled their faces and spilled over into their words. "Entice the man Samson," they said. "See wherein his great strength lies, and by what means we may prevail against him. We will give thee every one of us eleven hundred pieces of silver."

Delilah's eyes glistened with greed. Such a paltry task! Was not Samson already entrapped by her charms? Knowledge of her power over men made the proposition even more attractive. Eyes half-closed, she envisioned the velvets and silks, gold chains and rich jewels she would buy to enhance her perfumed body that drove men to madness.

When Samson came to her, Delilah began her campaign against the man who loved her. "Tell me," she began. "Where does it come from, the strength you possess? Should one wish to afflict you, how could it be done?"

Samson caressed her smooth cheek. "If I were bound with seven green cords that were never dried, I should be weak and be as another man."

Delilah promptly reported the answer to the lords of the Philistines. They brought her the seven green cords that had not been dried. Men lay in wait inside her chamber, and when Delilah bound Samson, she cried, "The Philistines be upon thee, Samson!"

He sprang to his feet, breaking the cords as if they had been single threads.

Delilah's face resembled a thundercloud. "Why do you mock me and lie to me? Tell me the truth, Samson."

This time he told her if his enemies bound him with new ropes that had never been used, he would be weak. She bound him, called out, and grew enraged when he broke them as easily as he had the green cords. Again she asked the secret of his strength, chagrined to find the power she thought she had over him had not yet been his undoing. Images of the vast fortune she had been promised faded.

Fury burned within her. It should not be so! She bound his locks, fastened them with a pin and watched Samson once more effortlessly free himself.

With tears and cajoling, Delilah vexed Samson until he told her all his heart. "There hath not come a razor upon my head; I have been a Nazarite unto God from my mother's womb: If I be shaven, then my strength will go from me, and I shall become weak and be like any other man."

Delilah felt torn between hope and the fear it was only another lie, but she reported to the Philistines, who brought the promised money. She made Samson sleep; a man came and shaved the luxuriant, uncut hair. This time when she cried, "The Philistines be upon thee," Samson awoke and said, "I will go out as at other times before, and shake myself." He did not know the Lord was departed from him. The Philistines took him away, leaving Delilah to gloat over her ill-gotten treasure.

No record is given of Delilah from that time forward. Historians can only speculate as to whether remorse filled her shallow, wicked soul when the Philistines put out Samson's eyes, bound him with fetters of brass, and brought him to Gaza. There he ground in the prison house, a beast of burden. His hair began to grow, as did his repentance.

Delilah may well have been one the Philistine men and women who made sport of Samson and praised their gods for delivering him into their hands. If so, she died with Samson and the others when God heard Samson's prayer, "O Lord God, remember me. . . and strengthen me, I pray thee only this once, O God, that I may be avenged of the Philistines for my two eyes." Taking hold of the middle pillars that held up the house, he pushed with all the restored might given by God. The walls crashed down, slaying the scheming lords and all with them.

NAOMI

RUTH 1–4

"Naomi, beloved." Elimelech turned a face filled with trouble toward his wife. "We cannot tarry in Bethlehem-judah any longer." Despair darkened his eyes. "Famine in our land continues, nay, grows stronger every day. We must take our sons and journey to the country of Moab. There we shall have—"

"Moab?" His good wife stared in disbelief. "Have you gone mad, my husband?" She glanced through the open doorway to where Mahlon and Chilion sat just out of hearing. "Where among the Moabites will our sons find proper wives?" Fear blanched her face and crept into her eyes. "Elimelech, this thing cannot be. Surely we must remain in our own country. Moab is filled with those who worship strange gods."

"There is food in Moab," her husband reminded. "To stay here is to starve." His gaze softened. "I like this journey no more than you, Naomi."

She said no more, but her mother's heart protested every mile of the way from Bethlehem-judah to the country of Moab, where they must sojourn. Heavy of spirit, she prayed the famine would end and they might return home. Instead, they were forced to continue in a strange land, living among those who worshipped heathen gods.

During their stay, Elimelech died, leaving Naomi bereft and alone with her two sons. Her worst fears came to pass when Mahlon and Chilion took wives of the women of Moab. Although Ruth and Orpah were comely, they were of a different faith, which sorely grieved Naomi.

Ten years later, Mahlon and Chilion also died. Naomi rocked with grief. Why had Jehovah taken first husband, then sons? Now only the two daughters-in-law remained. What should she do? Word had come that the Lord had visited His people in the land of Judah and ended the famine. Her heart yearned within her. Oh, to return to her own country. Even the thought of it cheered her sad heart. Naomi made her choice. No longer would she dwell among those who worshipped false gods and bowed down to images of wood and stone.

The day of departure came. Although she had learned to love Orpah and Ruth, Naomi well knew the young women would surely wish to marry. Better for them to remain in the land of Moab and find husbands among their own people. Naomi told them, "Go, return each to her mother's house: The Lord deal kindly with you, as ye have dealt with the dead, and with me. The Lord grant you that ye may find rest, each of you in the house of her husband." She kissed them.

Orpah and Ruth lifted up their voices and wept, saying, "Surely we will return with thee unto thy people."

Naomi shook her head. She told them they must stay. She had no husband, no more sons to offer as husbands for Orpah and Ruth. Even if she were to marry and bear sons, there would be far too many years before they grew into manhood.

Tears fell but Orpah at last accepted the parting. She kissed Naomi. Still weeping, she went back to her people and her gods. Ruth remained behind, cleaving unto the mother-in-law she loved more than life itself. Naomi could deny her no more. Together they started up the dusty road to Bethlehem.

RUTH

RUTH 1–4

"I have no son to be your husband," Naomi repeated to her tearful Moabite daughters-in-law.

Ruth scarcely heard her. Now that her husband lay in the grave, only Naomi remained to remind her of the happy years they had shared. She grew aware Orpah kissed the older woman and started back to her mother's house, as Naomi had told them to do. A wave of pain washed through her. She could not, would not let her mother-in-law go without her.

Ruth fell to her knees before Naomi. She flung her arms around the other's legs and pleaded, "Intreat me not to leave thee, or to return from following after thee: For whither thou goest, I will go; and where thou lodgest, I will lodge: Thy people shall be my people, and thy God my God.

"Where thou diest, will I die, and there will I be buried: The Lord do so to me, and more also, if ought but death part thee and me."

In the silence that fell, Ruth held her breath, asking The God of her husband to soften her mother-in-law's heart. Gradually the stiffness of Naomi's body melted. With great joy, Ruth caught the words she had so longed to hear. "Arise, my child. We shall go to Bethlehem-judah together."

They spoke no more of Ruth's impassioned plea, and when they reached Bethlehem in the beginning of barley harvest, Naomi told those about them, "Call me not Naomi, but Mara, for the Almighty hath dealt very bitterly with me. I went out full, and the Lord hath brought me home again empty."

Ruth begged to go into the fields and glean ears of corn that they might have food. She came to land belonging to Boaz, a mighty man of wealth and a kinsman of Elimelech. Ruth heard words of praise for Boaz from many and counted herself fortunate to follow the reapers in his fields. She also secretly rejoiced when he sought her out.

"Daughter, go not to glean in another field. . .abide here by my maidens. I have charged the young men not to touch thee. Drink of the vessels which they have drawn when thou thirst."

Ruth fell to the ground. "Why have I found grace in thine eyes, that thou should take knowledge of me, a stranger?"

Boaz told her he knew all she had done for her mother-in-law, that she had left her own father, mother, and land of nativity to come to a strange country. Ruth's heart stirred within her, the first time since the death of her husband. The comfort he offered showed she had found favor in his sight. She happily worked, not knowing Boaz had commanded his reapers to leave handfuls for her to glean.

Day after day Ruth gleaned in the fields, first barley, then wheat. Day after day she learned to admire Boaz more. When Naomi instructed her to wash and anoint herself and steal into the tent of Boaz while he lay sleeping, then uncover his feet and lie at them, she tremblingly obeyed. Boaz awakened to find her there. He told her to tarry the night, and if the one who was a nearer kinsman than he would not take her to wife, then would he do this thing.

All night Ruth lay sleepless, hoping the other man would refuse her. To her great joy, that kinsman drew off his shoe and sold all that belonged to Elimelech, Mahlon, and Chilion to Boaz. Boaz proclaimed to the necessary witnesses that Ruth would be his wife.

On the day of the marriage feast, Ruth remembered her vow to Naomi and silently repeated it in her heart, only this time to her husband. She would truly make his lodge, his people, his God, her own. Happiness filled her. It increased when the Lord blessed Boaz and her with a son. Naomi took the child, laid it in her bosom, and became nurse unto it. But Ruth praised the God of Israel she had come to know and called her son Obed, which means "worshipping God."

BOAZ

RUTH

Boaz was a wealthy man in Bethlehem during the time of the Old Testament judges. His romance and marriage to the Moabite widow Ruth is a heartwarming story of how God cares for His people in seemingly circuitous ways.

It did not take long for Boaz to notice the young stranger in his field gathering bits of grain left by his reapers. He knew this was Ruth, the foreign woman who had won the admiration of the Israelites because of her steadfast devotion in caring for her mother-in-law Naomi, for whom she was gathering the remnants of grain.

Naomi was a Jewish woman who, with her husband Elimelech and their sons, had been forced out of Bethlehem by famine. They settled in the land of Moab. There Elimelech—who was a relative of Boaz—died as did his two sons. When Naomi determined to return to her native Bethlehem, Ruth, one of her widowed daughters-in-law, vowed to come and care for her. Ruth disagreed with Naomi's reasoning that Ruth would fare better by remaining in her own land. "Wherever you go I will go," said Ruth. "Wherever you live I will live. Your people will be my people and your God will be my God."

And so the two women returned to Bethlehem where Boaz not only allowed Ruth to pick up the leftover grain, he took her under his wing, as well. He invited her to eat with him and privately instructed his workers to make sure there was plenty of grain for her to gather.

It occurred to Naomi that Boaz and Ruth would be a likely, godly match. She conspired to make Ruth the focus of Boaz's attention, and a mutual interest evolved between Boaz and Ruth.

Then Boaz found a novel way to secure their union. There was one man in Bethlehem who was a closer relative of Elimelech than was Boaz. By law this man had the right to buy from Naomi the land that had belonged to her husband. So Boaz arranged a meeting with the man. Ten elders of the town were present as witnesses. Boaz proposed that if the man wanted to buy the land he should do so; otherwise, Boaz would buy it.

"Of course I will buy it," the relative replied.

But Boaz pointed out that if the relative acquired the land, he also was obligated to marry Ruth. Their children would inherit the land, and thus the land would legally remain in the family of Ruth's dead husband, Mahlon, Elimelech's son. This the relative could not do, because it would create complications involving other property he owned. Boaz, he decided, could buy the land—and marry Ruth!

So the faithful Ruth and her long-suffering mother-in-law were well provided for. Boaz and Ruth had a son and named him Obed. Obed was the father of Jesse, the father of King David.

HANNAH

1 SAMUEL 1–2

Hannah, wife of Elkanah, mourned. She knew she had her husband's best love. He had given her a worthy portion of the yearly sacrifice, far more than that bestowed on his second wife, Peninnah, or to all her sons and daughters. If only she, wife of Elkanah's heart, could also give him children! Yet year after year when the family went up to the house of the Lord, Peninnah provoked Hannah until she wept and did not eat.

Elkanah said, "Hannah, why weepest thou? and why eatest thou not? and why is thy heart grieved? am not I better to thee than ten sons?"

She took comfort, but sought out Eli, the priest, who sat by a post of the temple of the Lord. In bitterness of soul, she prayed and wept. She vowed that if the Lord of hosts would give her a man-child, she would give him unto the Lord all the days of his life, and no razor would come upon his head.

Hannah spoke in her heart; her lips only moved. Eli thought her drunk. Hannah quickly denied it. "No, my lord. . .I have drunk neither wine nor strong drink but have poured out my soul before the Lord."

Eli told her to go in peace. The God of Israel would grant her petition. Hannah went her way. She ate, and sadness left her countenance.

Hannah conceived and bore a son. She called his name Samuel, saying, "Because I have asked him of the Lord." She did not go up to offer the yearly sacrifice and told Elkanah that when Samuel was weaned she would bring him before the Lord where the child would abide forever. At that time, Hannah took the child to Eli, the priest, repeating her vow and dedicating Samuel to God. She praised God, saying none was holy as the Lord and telling how her heart rejoiced.

Eli blessed Elkanah and Hannah, and the Lord visited her. She bore three sons and two daughters. The child Samuel grew before the Lord, bringing greater rejoicing than ever to his mother's heart as he ministered unto the Lord before Eli the priest.

When Samuel was still a lad, the Lord called him three times. Samuel did not yet know the Lord, neither was the word of the Lord yet revealed to him. He ran to Eli, who told him after the third time that if the voice came again, he should say, "Speak, Lord, for Thy servant hearest." Samuel did as instructed and the Lord told him many things, including that Eli would be judged for the iniquity of his sons. Samuel hesitated to tell his friend, but Eli insisted.

Eli only replied, "It is the Lord: let Him do what seemeth Him good."

Samuel grew, and the Lord was with him. All Israel from Dan even to Beersheba knew Samuel was established to be a prophet of the Lord.

As gracious as the meaning of her name, Hannah continued faithful. Surely in her secret mother's heart she missed and yearned for the son God gave her; the son she returned to a life of service in fulfillment of her vow. Hannah wisely overcame her longings with praise and a continual song before the Lord, telling of His power and goodness. Her song was handed down throughout the ages and remains a shining testimony of pure mother love transcended only by love of the Lord God of Israel, Almighty and Everlasting.

SAMUEL

1 AND 2 SAMUEL

Eli the high priest was almost blind when he was given a little boy named Samuel to raise in Shiloh. Samuel served him well, but Eli's own sons—priests like their father—were selfish and disrespectful of God. God determined to punish the family.

One night while Samuel was sleeping, the Lord called him by name. Samuel thought the voice he heard must be Eli's, so he rose and went to Eli's bedside. "What do you need?" he asked the priest.

"I didn't call you," Eli said grumpily. "Go back to sleep."

After Samuel had settled into his bedding, the Lord called his name again. Again he went to Eli and asked, "What do you want?" And again the agitated priest sent Samuel back to bed.

When it happened a third time and Samuel appeared at his bedside, Eli realized God was calling Samuel. "Go back to bed," Eli told him. "If you hear the voice, say 'I hear You, Lord. What do You want?'"

Samuel did as he was told, and the Lord gave him a dreadful message. God said that Eli and his family were going to be punished forever because of the disrespect of Eli's sons. Understandably, Samuel did not want to share this news with his mentor. But Eli demanded to know what God had said to him. So Samuel relayed the prophecy to him.

"He is God," Eli acknowledged sadly. "He will do the right thing."

As Samuel grew to manhood, God appeared to him with more messages. The people realized Samuel was God's prophet. In fact, Samuel became the last great judge of the Israelites.

Samuel made judges of his own sons. But like the sons of Eli, they were ungodly. The Israelites did not want to follow them, and they demanded that Samuel in his old age appoint a king to rule the nation. This was not what the Lord wanted. Samuel warned them but they insisted. So Samuel anointed a king for them. His name was Saul.

For a time, Saul was a good leader who protected his people. But eventually he turned away from God. Then God told Samuel, "I'm sorry I made Saul king of My people." He sent Samuel to the house of Jesse to find another king. Jesse's youngest son, David, would become Israel's greatest leader, but he was just a boy when Samuel privately anointed him to succeed the reigning King Saul.

SAUL

1 SAMUEL 9–31

The young man Saul, son of Kish, was a head taller than any other Israelite. This handsome young man was introduced to Samuel, the prophet/judge who would bring him to power. Saul and his servant were looking for some escaped donkeys and were on the verge of giving up. The servant suggested they find the prophet Samuel and see if he could point them to their donkeys.

Samuel did much more than that. With a jar of olive oil, he anointed Saul king of the land! The Holy Spirit took hold of Saul, and he danced and shouted.

At first, Saul diligently sought the Lord's guidance and victoriously led the Israelites into battle against their enemies. But on one critical occasion, he failed to follow God's instructions carefully, and it cost him his kingship.

Samuel told Saul that God wanted to punish the Amalekites for their past opposition to the Hebrews. "Attack them and destroy them," Samuel ordered the king. "Leave none of them, young or old, alive. Kill even the babies. Kill all their domestic animals, too."

Saul's soldiers attacked and slaughtered the Amalekites and took their king prisoner. But Saul failed to carry out God's command. He let the heathen king live. Moreover, his men killed only the weakest sheep and cattle and held back the choicest livestock, ostensibly to offer as sacrifices to the Lord.

God was very displeased with Saul. He had given Saul victory over Israel's longtime enemy, and Saul had responded with disobedience. God sent Samuel to inform the king that God hereby rejected him. God then sent the prophet to secretly anoint David as the future successor.

Saul brought the youthful David into his service as a court musician. David soon won the heart of the nation in his famous encounter with the Philistine giant Goliath. Saul became paranoid and jealous of David. He sensed that the young man might take his place and wanted to kill him. Soon, David and his growing legions of followers were driven into exile by King Saul.

Interestingly, it wasn't David or any of his men who ultimately ended Saul's life. In fact, David on more than one occasion let Saul live when he easily could have killed his tormentor. Saul and his sons died in a battle against Israel's fierce rivals, the Philistines. Although it brought his persecution to an end, Saul's death did not make David happy. Rather, he wrote a heartrending lament for Saul.

JONATHAN

1 SAMUEL 13:3–4; 13:16–14:46; 18:1–4; 19:1–7;
20; 23:16–18; 31:1–5; 2 SAMUEL 1:1–27

How hard it must be to have a friend who is also your father's enemy—especially if your father is the most powerful man in the country. This was Jonathan's predicament. When the young shepherd David killed Goliath, Saul, king of Israel, brought David into his service. At that time Jonathan, Saul's son, gave David his clothing and armor as tokens, and they became loyal friends.

Jonathan's allegiance soon saved David's life. Saul knew the Lord loved David and was afraid God would replace him with the youngster. David won many battles over the Philistines, Israel's great foe, and his popularity disturbed Saul and stirred his jealousy. He became obsessed with the thought of killing David. Jonathan tried to change Saul's mind by gently reminding him of David's valuable service. Saul agreed not to hurt David—but this promise soon was forgotten.

Saul's anger toward David became uncontrollable, so Jonathan stepped in to help David escape. Jonathan knew David was going to become king, and he wanted to serve as David's right-hand man. They swore before God to always be loyal and helpful to each other and to each other's family.

Sadly this was not to be. In a battle against the Philistines at Mount Gilboa, Saul was killed along with Jonathan and two of Saul's other sons. David grieved long for Jonathan and even for the relentless Saul. David wrote "The Song of the Bow" about Saul and Jonathan and required that everyone in Judah learn it. To David, Jonathan was his brother, and he lamented the loss of such a faithful friend.

DAVID

1 SAMUEL 16:1–1 KINGS 2:11

David was the greatest of Israel's kings. His forty-year reign was a roller coaster of amazing gains and foolish losses, exemplary leadership and shocking failure. Yet he was a man after God's own heart.

The great prophet Samuel was dispatched to the house of Jesse in Bethlehem. One of Jesse's sons was to succeed Saul as king of Israel. One by one Jesse paraded his seven older sons before Samuel. But God told Samuel to reject each of them. Finally Jesse called for his youngest son, David, a hardy, sunburned shepherd. "Anoint him," God told Samuel, and God's Spirit came upon David—and left King Saul. David soon entered Saul's service as a musician, playing his harp to soothe the king's troubled mind.

David's most famous act occurred at this time. The Philistine army was gathered to fight the Israelites near Shochoh. Each day Goliath, the giant soldier of the Philistines, strutted from the Philistine camp and taunted the Israelites camped across the valley. He challenged the bravest of them to come out and fight him. The Jewish soldiers, including David's own brothers, knew the giant could not be beaten, so they cowered in disgrace.

One day David arrived in camp with food for his brothers. "Who is this uncircumcised enemy who defies the army of the Lord?" he demanded and immediately asked Saul for permission to take on the giant. Understandably, Saul refused because of David's youth, modest size, and inexperience. But David pointed out that as a shepherd he had killed a lion and a bear when they had raided his flock. And in any case, David knew the Lord would protect him. The king assented.

Declining Saul's heavy sword and armor, David selected a few smooth stones from a brook and, sling in hand, approached the haughty giant. Goliath, angry that the Israelites had sent a boy with no sword or armor to fight him, cursed the youth. "I will feed your flesh to the animals," he snarled.

David replied, "You come to me with heavy weapons, but I come to you in God's name. Today I'm going to take your head, and your army will be defeated, for this is the Lord's battle."

And so it happened. One stone hurled from David's sling was all it took. Struck solidly in the forehead, Goliath fell on his face, killed instantly. David chopped off Goliath's head with the giant's own sword, and the Israelites attacked and routed the demoralized Philistines.

For the rest of his life—while fleeing from jealous Saul to the years of his own kingship—David sought the Lord's will. His love and reverence for God live today in many of the psalms he penned. But other psalms speak from deepest human despair, for David frequently was tested. He also made serious mistakes. His lust for Bathsheba, for example, led him not only to adultery but to conspire to commit murder.

He also was one of the most incompetent parents in Scripture. He loved his sons passionately but could not bring himself to discipline them. Tragedy upon tragedy resulted, first with Amnon, then with Absalom and Adonijah.

David designated his son Solomon to succeed him as king and instructed him just before death. This advice elucidates David's character: "Obey the Lord your God. Walk in His ways, and keep His laws."

MICHAL

1 SAMUEL 18–19; 2 SAMUEL 3, 6

Michal, younger daughter of King Saul, loved David from the time she first saw him. Yet she knew she must lay her love aside. Her father had promised David the hand of Merab, his elder daughter. All of Michal's inner rebellion could not change things. She considered going to her father but hastily put aside the thought. Everyone knew of the rages that came upon Saul. Michal shuddered. She dared not chance having his wrath turned toward her.

Much had happened since the day David, son of Jesse, first stood before Saul. Ruddy, goodly to look on, his beautiful countenance attracted both Saul and young Michal. The king sent to Jesse, saying, "Let David stand before me; for he hath found favor in my sight."

From that time on when the evil spirit entered Saul, David played softly on his harp. The music soothed the king, refreshed him, and he became well. Saul loved David greatly and made him his armor bearer.

Michal sighed. When did the corrosion of envy begin to enter Saul's heart, leaving it open to the evil spirit that vexed him? She sadly shook her head. Perhaps when the young shepherd went forth against the mighty Philistine Goliath. A tender look of remembrance crossed Michal's face, and a smile curved her lips. David had thrown aside the king's own armor, a helmet of brass and a coat of mail. Taking five smooth stones and his sling, he slew the giant.

How her father had praised him—then. Michal thrilled at David's bravery, as she had scores of times before. She thought how her own brother Jonathan's very soul knit with the soul of David. Her dark eyes glowed. Jonathan had stripped himself of garments, sword, and bow and given them to David as a token of the covenant of brotherhood between them.

Sadness replaced Michal's smile. Saul set David over his soldiers, and all Israel and Judah loved David. A pang of fear went through her. She had seen her father's anger when the new young leader returned from the slaughter of the Philistines. Women came out of all the cities of Israel, singing and dancing, saying as they played on instruments, "Saul hath slain his thousands, and David his ten thousands."

The next day while in the throes of an evil spirit, Saul threw a javelin and barely missed killing the young man he had loved until mistrust changed everything. He grew afraid of David because the Lord was with him and had departed from Saul. The king made him captain over a thousand and sent him from his presence. At that time, Saul also promised Merab to David.

Michal felt hot shame when her father broke his vow and gave Merab to another but could not deny the spirit of joy that rose within when Saul decided to give her to David instead. Nothing could make her happier.

Saul, the man God had called to reign over His people, had changed into a treacherous, bitter king. Jonathan stood between father and friend, true to his vow. Michal saved her husband's life when Saul's men came after him by letting him down through a window. She put the form of a man in her bed and said David lay sick when Saul sent messengers to take him.

Did Michal's heart break when her father gave her as wife to Phalti after David became an outlaw? And when David took first Abigail, then Ahinoam, as his wives? After Saul's death and David's anointing as king of Judah, he demanded Michal be returned to him. The Bible says her weeping husband went with her until he was sent back.

What memories filled the heart that had once been wholly David's? It appears love fled sometime over the years. Michal railed against David when she saw him leaping and dancing in front of the people. He responded by reminding her he was the king, chosen by the Lord. He vowed to be even more vile. No wonder God had to give David a new heart before the shepherd who became king could change into the man God needed.

Michal had no children by David.

ABIGAIL

Few men were more blessed than Nabal. He owned three thousand sheep and a thousand goats. In addition, his wife Abigail not only had a beautiful countenance but possessed good understanding. Nabal should have sung praises for all that was his as he sheared his sheep in Carmel. The churlish man did not and was known for his evil doings.

David, in the wilderness, mourning for Samuel's death, heard of Nabal. He called out ten young men and said, "Get you up to Carmel, and go to Nabal, and greet him in my name." He went on to tell them to extend peace to Nabal and his house and all he had and to remind Nabal how well David had treated the shepherds while they were in Carmel.

David finished his instructions by telling the young men to say, "Give, I pray thee, whatsoever cometh to thine hand unto thy servants, and to thy son David."

Nabal listened to the words of David as given by the young men then sneered. "Who is David? and who is the son of Jesse? there be many servants nowadays that break away every man from his master. Shall I then take my bread, and my water, and my flesh that I have killed for my shearers, and give it unto men, whom I know not whence they be?"

This angered David greatly. He ordered four hundred of his men to gird themselves with their swords and follow him.

One of the young men who served Nabal witnessed the exchange. He told Abigail how David sent messengers out of the wilderness to salute the master but that Nabal railed against them. He went on to tell her of David and his men's kindness and protection to Nabal's shepherds when they were in the field. Nothing of Nabal's was missing during all the time they tended the sheep. "They were a wall unto us both by night and day, all the while we were with them keeping the sheep," he earnestly reported. "Know and consider what thou wilt do; for evil is determined against our master, and against all of his household: For he is such a son of Belial* that a man cannot speak to him."

Anger at her husband's treatment of David's messengers surged through Abigail. She immediately took great quantities of food and loaded it on asses. She said nothing of her plan to Nabal but followed her servants. Heart beating in time with the hooves of the ass she rode, she came down the hill and met David and his followers. Abigail dismounted and fell pleading at his feet to beg mercy. She told him she had been given no knowledge of the rude way his men were treated and offered the food she had brought. She prophesied of the great things the Lord God of Israel would one day do with David.

David rejoiced that Abigail had kept him from shedding blood. He sent her to her house in peace. She found Nabal holding a great feast and drunken with wine. She told him nothing until the next day. His heart failed when he heard those things, and ten days later he died.

Abigail later became David's wife. The mists of time obscure most of her life after that. We know she was one of many wives, bore a son called Chileab, was taken captive by the Amalekites, then rescued by David. Did she maintain the high courage that first brought her to David's attention? The beautiful countenance? Or did years of having to share her husband with other women slowly grind her down? The story of how she lived up to the meaning of her name, "of strength," serves as an example of one unafraid to face the enemy and conquer by reasoning, rather than by the use of weapons.

---

*Belial: wicked, worthless

JOAB

2 SAMUEL 2:8–3:39; 8:15–18; 10:1–14; 11:1–25; 12:26–27;
14:1–33; 18:1–19:7; 20:6–23; 1 KINGS 1:1–2:35;
1 CHRONICLES 11:6–8; 19:8–15; 20:1; 21:1–7

Civil war was brewing. King Saul was dead, and the people of Judah wanted David to be their king. Meanwhile to the north in Israel, the army commander Abner had made Saul's son Ishbosheth a puppet king; Abner himself held the real power. Men who once respected each other had become enemies.

Joab and his brothers Abishai and Asahel were warriors for David. But Abner killed Joab's brother Asahel, and Joab was angered when Abner made a pact with David. Without David's knowledge, Joab arranged a meeting with Abner and murdered him in cold blood. Dismayed, David ordered his people to mourn for Abner and prayed that God would punish Joab and his family.

This set the tone of David and Joab's relationship. When David became king of all Israel, Joab was the commander of his army. Joab proved to be a clever, brave military leader who always wanted to do what he thought was best for David. But he sometimes did things his own way and was never afraid to speak his mind to the king. For example, David's rebellious son Absalom tried to take over the kingship. A battle ensued and David wanted his soldiers to let Absalom live. But Joab knew David's softheartedness would only result in future trouble with Absalom. So, while Absalom hung by his hair, helpless in a tree, Joab killed him.

At the end of David's reign, Joab allied himself with David's son Adonijah who wanted to take over the throne. David instead chose his son Solomon to succeed him. On his deathbed David cited Joab's disrespect to Solomon. "Punish him as you will," David said. "Do not let him die in peace."

Solomon wasted little time securing his position as king. He dispatched Benaiah, who had been the captain of David's bodyguard and would become Solomon's army commander, to kill Adonijah and Joab. And so, this clever player in the game of politics and war ultimately was paid in violence for his choices.

NATHAN

2 SAMUEL 7:1–17; 12:1–15, 24–25; 1 KINGS 1:10–45;
1 CHRONICLES 17:1–15; 29:29; 2 CHRONICLES 9:29; 29:25

W hy have you trampled on the Lord's laws and done this evil?" said the prophet to the king. This booming indictment came in response to a serious deed that called into question the sinner's regard for God Almighty. Few people would have the nerve to talk to a king this way. But Nathan the prophet knew that the sin of King David was so great the hills would have roared in anguish had it gone unreproved.

David fell in love with Bathsheba, the wife of a Hittite warrior named Uriah who fought in David's army. Not only so, David had committed adultery with Bathsheba. To lawfully remove Bathsheba's husband so he could marry her, David ordered Joab, the commander of his army, to place Uriah in the thick of battle. Then, to make doubly sure Uriah died, David had his general arrange for the army to withdraw suddenly and leave Uriah alone against the enemy. This was nothing short of murder. After Uriah's death, David took the widow Bathsheba for his wife.

The prophet Nathan became aware of the king's sinfulness and soon arrived in the palace to tell David this story: A rich man owned many cows and sheep. In the same town a poor man lived who owned just one little lamb. The lamb meant a lot to the poor man and his family. In fact, it was their pet. One day the rich man began to prepare a banquet, but he did not want to kill any of his own animals for the meal. So he stole the poor man's lamb, cooked it, and served it to his guests.

David was furious at the fictitious rich man. Then Nathan interpreted, "You are that rich man."

Nathan told David that because of his bloody treachery with Uriah and Bathsheba, David's own family would reap a bloody reward. "This will never again be a peaceful house," Nathan promised.

David repented, and the Lord did not punish him by death. But the newborn son, conceived in David and Bathsheba's adultery, did not live.

BATHSHEBA

2 SAMUEL 11–12; 1 KINGS 2

W hat shall I do?" The distraught woman hugged her arms across her breast and rocked to and fro. Fear smote her, tasting metallic in her mouth. "I shall be stoned, even though the king himself be responsible for my plight." The thought settled her whirling brain. Hope crept over into troubled face. Surely David would not allow such a thing to happen! Making haste, she sent a message by a trusted servant, four short words.

King David curiously opened the missive and read, "I am with child." He laid it aside, remembering. After the year of peace that had been declared, he sent Joab, his servants, and all Israel forth to battle, but David tarried at Jerusalem. One eveningtide, he arose from his bed to walk on the roof of his house. He looked down from his lofty domain, and his blood ran hot, for a lovely woman washed herself. He must discover who she was.

"Bathsheba, wife of Uriah the Hittite," came the reply.

Her married status could not quell the fire of David's desire. He commanded that she be brought to him. Now she had conceived. What could he do? Even a king was not exempt from the punishment for adultery, which was death.

A scheme formed in his mind. He would bring Uriah back from fighting and send him to his wife so that the evil David had done might not be discovered.

David's plan did not work. Uriah came but slept at the door of the king's house with the servants. A conscientious soldier, he would not go to his home and wife while the ark of the covenant and his master Joab and fellow companions camped in the open fields.

David hastily sent him back to Joab, carrying a letter that ordered the commander to put Uriah in the forefront of the hottest battle and leave him there to be smitten and die. Joab obeyed and it came to pass.

Bathsheba mourned for the husband she had lost, guilt-ridden, secretly glad he never knew that which had come upon her. When her mourning time ended, David took her as his wife. But the thing David had done displeased the Lord.

Fear again filled Bathsheba when Nathan posed a riddle to the king that showed clearly he knew on whose order Uriah had died. Nathan made a terrible pronouncement: Evil would rise against David out of his own house, and all Israel would know.

The child Bathsheba had borne unto David fell ill and on the seventh day died. Her mother's heart filled with anguish. This, then, was the price to be paid for sin. Not until David comforted her and she bore another son, called Solomon, did Bathsheba's sad heart find joy again. Years later, when David was old, she fought for her son Solomon to be named king in place of Adonijah, who even then was taking over, for David was stricken in years and knew not what was happening. People were crying, "God save King Adonijah." King David swore by the Lord God of Israel that Solomon would sit on the throne in his stead. He ordered Solomon to be anointed as ruler over Israel and Judah.

Bathsheba bowed with her face to the earth. Triumph filled her soul. She did reverence to the king and said, "Let my lord King David live for ever."

After David's death, Solomon ascended to the throne. Adonijah sought her out, saying he came in peace. He asked her to intercede with King Solomon that he might be given Abishag, David's Shunammite concubine, as his wife.

Bathsheba agreed. Solomon seated her at his right hand but grew enraged when she made the request. He told her she might as well have asked the kingdom and ordered that Adonijah be executed unless he bowed down to the rightful king, which he did. Nothing more is known of Bathsheba.

SOLOMON

1 KINGS 1–11; PROVERBS; ECCLESIASTES;
THE SONG OF SOLOMON

G od spoke to the new king in a dream, "Tell Me what you
wish." The king was already awed by the enormity of his new
responsibility. He realized that he was very young to be the ruler of
Israel. "Give me wisdom," he prayed, "so I can rule wisely and always
know right from wrong." God was pleased with this humble, mature
request. "I will make you wiser than anyone who has ever lived or
anyone yet to be born," He promised.

This new king was Solomon, son of David. Early in his reign he
had the opportunity to display this God-given wisdom. Two women
who lived in the same house each had an infant son. One of the
babies was accidentally smothered to death, and both women claimed
to be the mother of the surviving child. They appeared before the
king for a judgment.

"Bring a sword and cut the living child in half," Solomon
ordered. "Give each woman a half of the child."

"No! Please don't kill him!" one of the women cried. "Let her
take him!"

Solomon knew immediately this was the child's true mother.
She loved the baby so much she was willing to surrender him rather
than see him killed. He restored the infant to her. This deepened
respect for the king among the people.

Solomon built and furnished a majestic temple to God's honor
in Jerusalem, and Israel prospered greatly. This temple was the one
his father David had desired to build. Solomon built a beautiful,
ornate palace for himself. Even today people know of the wealth of
Solomon. He recognized that this wealth came from God and
prayed for the Lord's blessings over the Israelites.

Although wealth did not corrupt him—at least, not directly —
his lust for women did. The Bible says that Solomon had seven
hundred wives and three hundred mistresses. Many of them were

foreigners from the lands of Israel's enemies. God had forbidden the Israelites to intermarry. Predictably, some of these wives and concubines persuaded the aging king to worship their own heathen gods.

Solomon's sinful way soon would be punished by civil war among the Hebrew tribes. Despite all this, because of his love for Solomon's father, David, God pledged to let Solomon remain in power until the day he died.

The Queen
of Sheba

1 Kings 10

Solomon's fame spread to the uttermost ends of the known earth. Tales of his wealth and wisdom ran far and wide. People spoke of his wisdom that came about in this manner:

In Gibeon the Lord appeared to Solomon in a dream and said, "Ask what I shall give thee."

Solomon rehearsed the great mercy God had shown to his father, David, according to when he walked in truth, righteousness, and uprightness of heart. God had kept for David great kindness, even a son to sit on his throne.

"I am but a little child," Solomon confessed. "I know not how to go out or come in. Thy servant is in the midst of Thy people which Thou hast chosen, a great people, that cannot be numbered nor counted for multitude. Give therefore Thy servant an understanding heart to judge Thy people, that I may discern between good and bad: For who is able to judge this Thy so great a people?"

The request pleased God. He promised that since Solomon had not asked wealth or long life or the life of his enemies, there would be none like Solomon either before or after. God also blessed Solomon abundantly with the riches he had not sought, with honor and length of days.

In faraway Arabia, the queen of Sheba rested on soft cushions and narrowed her painted eyelids. Who was this Solomon, this man whose praise was sung by every passing caravan? She surveyed her surroundings. Did he, then, possess more than she? Was his palace more splendid, his robes of grander fabric and design? She laughed, mocking the thought. Did not the world know none was so mighty as the queen of Sheba?

Yet a note of jealousy marred the laugh and with it came a daring idea. Why should she not go to Jerusalem and see for herself? A single clap of the hands would bring a bevy of servants ready to do her bidding. Stay. She must consider well before embarking on the journey.

The queen's curiosity waxed hotter with every wild tale. Even allowing for certain exaggeration, the kingdom of Solomon loomed ever more appealing in her mind. At last she ordered a great train to be prepared, camels bearing spices, quantities of gold, and precious stones. When she reached Jerusalem, she decked herself out in her finest apparel and came to Solomon.

Armed with questions, the queen shot them at the ruler whose fame had spread like fire in a field of ripe and waving wheat. Her all-seeing eyes saw the splendor of his house, the food, all who served him, even the way in which he went up unto the house of the Lord. She hated to admit defeat, but what she saw forced her to do so. She said, "I believed not the words until I came. . . Behold, the half was not told me: Thy wisdom and prosperity exceedeth the fame which I heard. Happy are thy men. . .thy servants which stand continually before thee, and that hear thy wisdom. Blessed be the Lord thy God, which delighted in thee, to set thee on the throne of Israel: Because the Lord loved Israel for ever, therefore made He thee king, to do judgment and justice."

The queen of Sheba gave Solomon great riches, but he gave her all her desire, whatsoever she asked, beside that which Solomon gave her of his royal bounty. She and her servants turned and went to her own country.

Scripture records that the magnificence of Solomon's court impressed the queen "until there was no more spirit in her." Perhaps this best shows the extent to which God blessed the king with material possessions. The magnitude of Solomon's wisdom, power, and honor cannot be measured.

JEZEBEL

1 KINGS 16, 18–19; 2 KINGS 9

A hab, son of Omri, reigned over Israel twenty and two years. It is written he "did evil in the sight of the Lord above all that were before him," surpassing the wickedness of anyone up to that time. Marrying Jezebel and embracing her gods ranked first on his list of sins.

The name Jezebel has been known throughout history as a synonym for dark deeds and treachery. It is not hard to picture a scene such as this:

Jezebel, silken, perfumed, jeweled, lolling on richly embroidered cushions. Painted face. Long fingernails stained as red as if dipped in blood. Physically beautiful enough to tempt any man not dedicated to a God higher than those she served. A hundred plots milling in her scheming, clever brain. A dozen maidens clustered around her, freakish imitations of Jezebel's sensuous charm.

"I will marry Ahab himself," she predicts. Her eyes glitter with assurance of her power over men. "I shall be queen of all Israel. What better way to establish the true religion, the worship of Baal?"

A murmur ripples through the bevy of maidens, but no one dares disagree. Jezebel's streak of cruelty and supreme vanity permit no criticism. She reigns her private kingdom by fear, not through admiration of those who serve and fawn upon her.

"Ahab shall build a house of Baal in Samaria and set up an altar to him." Jezebel whips herself into a frenzy. Hot color pours into her cheeks, and a gleam that spells disaster for anyone who gets in her way comes to her eyes. "Ahab shall also make a grove. . ." She allows her voice to trail off, and a self-satisfied smirk tilts her red, red lips.

The maidens clap their hands. Their eyes glisten. Only too well do they know the dancing, cavorting, and unholy actions in the groves dedicated to the heathen gods the Israelites despise. "Will such a thing not provoke the God of Ahab?" one, more daring than the rest, asks.

Affronted, Jezebel sternly reminds them, "There is no god like Baal." She sinks her white teeth into her painted lower lip and plans more evil.

How she rejoices when Ahab does as she asks! How she boasts. She cuts off the prophets of the Lord, all except the hundred Obadiah spirits away, hides in a cave, and feeds bread and water. She laughs at famine and drought, little caring that many suffer because of her and Ahab. She hates Elijah with all the fury of one who knows her own vileness but will not tolerate anyone speaking of it. If fear crosses her mind when he challenges her gods, she hides it and exultantly anticipates the confrontation on Mount Carmel between her 450 prophets of Baal and 400 of the grove. This day will Baal defeat the Israelite God forever!

It does not happen. All morning, the prophets cry for Baal to send fire and consume the offering on the altar. Nothing happens, even though they scream until hoarse and leap on the altar.

At noon Elijah mocks the false prophets, taunting that their gods must be asleep or talking or perhaps away on a journey. The priests slash their bodies, and Jezebel shrieks at them to conquer. That evening Elijah builds an altar in the name of the Lord. Three times it is soaked with water. After a simple prayer, fire comes from heaven and consumes everything, including the water in the trench. The people fall on their faces, crying, "The Lord, He is the God." Elijah slays every false prophet, and the rain returns.

Jezebel's fury knows no bounds when Ahab tells her what has happened. She threatens Elijah's life and laughs when he prophesies her violent end. Years later, vain to the last, she paints her face and taunts Jehu, the new king, from her window. Perhaps she feels her aging charms will save her. Is there regret in her heart when the eunuchs who sympathize with Jehu lift her up and throw her from the window? If so, is it for her wickedness or only her loss of power and life? No one knows. . .and as Elijah prophesied, the dogs wait below.

ELIJAH

Prophesies are not always ominous or kingdom shattering. In the instance of Elijah and the widow of Zarephath, the issue was providing food for a family.

Elijah met the woman at the city gate after obeying God's command to journey to Zarephath. There he requested of her water and bread. She responded that she was so poor that she had only a little flour and oil; she was planning to use the last of it to prepare a meal for herself and her son. After this she fully expected to starve to death. Elijah told her to prepare the meal as planned—but first to make him a little bread. When she did that he told her, "The Lord will see to it that your flour bin and oil jar remain full."

And, to the woman's amazement, this happened. A short time later her son became ill and died. In her anguish she questioned the fairness of Elijah and his God. So Elijah took the child upstairs and prayed for the child to be brought back to life. He stretched his body over the corpse, and God warmed the body and breathed life back into the boy. The woman could no longer doubt. "Now," she said, "I know you are a godly man, and the Lord has given you His truth to preach."

Other issues for this prophet from Gilead were significant on a national level. Elijah was a contemporary of King Ahab and wicked Queen Jezebel of the northern kingdom of Israel. Under Ahab, the people worshipped Baal instead of God.

Elijah, who in Ahab's words was the "troubler of Israel," challenged the king and his Baal-worshipping prophets to a contest on Mount Carmel. Crowds of Israelites stood by as witnesses. He proposed that two bulls be sacrificed by fire. Ahab's prophets would summon Baal to light the fire beneath their sacrifice, then Elijah would call on the name of the Lord to ignite his offering.

Elijah had great fun mocking the futile, frantic, protracted attempts of the heathen prophets to get Baal to do something—

anything at all. "Perhaps Baal is busy with other things," Elijah taunted, "or away on a trip. Maybe he's asleep and doesn't want to be bothered." All day long they tried to cajole Baal into lighting the fire. Of course, nothing happened. Finally they gave up.

When it was his turn, Elijah set up God's miracle with a flourish. He built an altar with twelve stones, symbolic of the twelve tribes of Israel. He dug a trench around it, laid on the wood, and put the meat of the bull on the wood. Then he ordered everything thoroughly drenched with water, making it seemingly impossible for a fire to burn. The trench surrounding the altar was filled with water. Elijah then prayed to God to turn the people's hearts back to Him.

God not only lit the wet altar but made the fire so intense it dried up the surrounding trench. The people were quite convinced. They rounded up the heathen prophets, and Elijah executed them.

When Queen Jezebel heard the news, she vowed to kill Elijah, and the remainder of the prophet's life was spent in tension and confrontation with Ahab and Jezebel, and their successor Ahaziah. Elijah performed dramatic miracles, which affirmed God's power and glory.

And Elijah did not die. Instead, as he was walking with the prophet Elisha, a chariot of fire appeared, and Elijah was carried upward in a whirlwind. Centuries later the apostles Peter, James, and John saw Elijah appear with Jesus at the Transfiguration, and the Bible tells us Elijah himself will return before the final judgment. Clearly, Elijah was a prophet of unique importance with a role to play in God's kingdom far beyond his earthly generation.

THE ZAREPHATH WIDOW

1 KINGS 17

Only a poor widow, her name is unknown to those who handed down her story from generation to generation. Yet the widow who dwelt in Zarephath is revered by all who meet her in the first book of Kings. She gave all. Not because she could afford to give. The widow could not afford not to give.

God sent ravens to feed Elijah during the famine by which he was punishing Israel, telling him to hide by the brook Cherith and drink from it. The brook dried up for lack of rain in the land, so God sent Elijah to Zarephath, saying, "I have commanded a widow woman there to sustain thee."

When Elijah reached the gate of the city, a widow woman bent low, gathering sticks. He called to her. "Fetch me, I pray thee, a little water in a vessel, that I may drink." She started to obey, and he called again, "Bring me I pray thee, a morsel of bread in thine hand."

The widow stared at him. If only she could! Offering water was one thing; sharing food another. Her thin hands trembled, and she thought of the final bit of food in her possession. "As the Lord thy God liveth, I have not a cake, but an handful of meal in a barrel, and a little oil in a cruse. . . . I am gathering two sticks that I may go in and dress it for me and my son, that we may eat it, and die."

"Fear not," Elijah told her. "Go and do as thou hast said; but make and bring me a little cake first, and after make for thee and for thy son. For thus saith the Lord God of Israel, 'The barrel of meal shall not waste, neither shall the cruse of oil fail, until the day that the Lord sendeth rain upon the earth.' "

The widow could scarcely believe her ears. Who was this stranger to promise such a thing? Was it a deception to gain the last of her food? She looked into his face. Something caused her to do his bidding. She slowly took out the meal and oil to make a cake for the stranger, but there yet remained other meal and oil. She marveled, prepared food for herself and her child, and thanked the God of Israel. For many days, each time the household hungered, the widow closed her eyes in fear, then rejoiced and baked cakes from the never-empty barrel and cruse.

Her blessings did not end with food. After these things, the widow's son fell ill until his breath left him. She called out in pain, asking why Elijah had done so unto her. He took the child to a loft and laid him upon the bed. He then cried to the Lord, stretched himself upon the child three times, and said, "O Lord my God, I pray thee, let this child's soul come into him again."

Elijah took the child, brought him down out of the chamber into the house, and delivered him unto his mother: And Elijah said, "See, thy son liveth."

The widow raised her head, bowed with weeping. She stilled her mourning and received her child with great joy. Her heart overflowed with gratefulness, and she said unto Elijah, "Now by this I know that thou art a man of God, and that the word of the Lord in thy mouth is truth."

And it all began with a handful of meal and a little oil in a cruse.

ELISHA

1 KINGS 19:15–21; 2 KINGS 2:1–8:15; 13:14–21

God chose Elisha to succeed Elijah as chief prophet in the ninth century B.C. Elisha was with Elijah when the great prophet was carried heavenward in the whirlwind. Then Elisha picked up the cloak Elijah left behind and went to the nearby Jordan River. Was the Lord empowering him to be the next prophet? When Elisha struck the water with the cloak, God opened a path for him to cross the river and confirmed his prophethood.

Elisha performed many miracles including the provision of an inexplicably boundless supply of oil that paid a widow's debts and the prophecy of a son for a childless woman in Shunem who indeed bore a son. But the boy died, and Elisha brought him back to life.

Another of Elisha's miracles was his feeding of a hundred men with a few loaves of bread, much like the Lord Jesus would feed the multitudes in a later era. Also like Jesus, Elisha healed the leper Naaman. And his uncanny knowledge repeatedly foiled the warring Arameans' attacks against Israel. Elisha always performed his miracles and prophecies to draw attention not to himself, but to God.

God honored this devotion, even beyond Elisha's death. An astonishing postscript to his story is recorded in 2 Kings 13:20–21. Sometime after the prophet's burial, some Israelites were in the process of another burial when they were interrupted by a band of Moabites. In their haste to escape the raiders, the burial party flung the corpse into Elisha's tomb. When the body touched the bones of the dead prophet, the man came back to life!

The story of this prophet/patriarch lives on to remind us that God can and does use dedicated believers as agents of His incredible power and goodness.

THE SHUNAMMITE WOMAN

2 KINGS 4

"S ir, I beg of you to eat bread with us," a woman of Shunem pleaded with Elisha when he came to her village.

Elisha turned aside and ate with the woman, who was highly respected by all who knew her. She immediately beseeched the prophet to honor her home by eating with them whenever he came to Shunem. And so Elisha ate at the woman's table.

The good woman perceived he was a holy man of God, who passed by continually. She told her husband, "Let us make a little chamber, I pray thee, on the wall; and let us set for him there a bed, and a table, and a stool, and a candlestick: And it shall be, when he cometh to us, that he shall turn in thither."

The next time Elisha came, he entered the chamber and lay there. After a time he ordered his servant Gehazi, "Call this Shunammite." When she stood before him, Elisha spoke of how carefully she had provided for him. He asked, "What is to be done for thee? wouldst thou be spoken for to the king, or to the captain of the host?"

"I dwell among my own people," she answered.

Again Elisha asked, "What then is to be done for her?"

Gehazi, who had remained silent during the interchange, spoke. "Verily she hath no child, and her husband is old."

For the second time Elisha called her. When the woman stood in the door he said, "About this season, according to the time of life, thou shalt embrace a son."

The woman stared at him, then shook her head. "Nay, my lord," she sadly replied. "Thou man of God, do not lie unto thine handmaid."

Great was her joy when, even as Elisha had predicted, she conceived and bore a son in due season.

One day when the child grew older, he went out to his father who was with the reapers. Suddenly he clutched his head and groaned.

"My head, my head!" Alarmed, his father ordered a lad to carry him to his mother. The stricken son sat on her knees till noon, then died. The good woman refused to accept his death. She laid him on Elisha's bed, shut the door, and went out. "Send me one of the young men," she ordered her grieving husband. "And one of the asses, that I may run to the man of God, and come again."

The husband couldn't understand. He asked why she would go on that day. But the great woman only said, "It shall be well." Commanding the young man driving the donkeys not to hesitate for her, she went and came unto Mount Carmel.

Gehazi, the servant, met her when she was yet afar off from the man of God. He told her Elisha had seen her and told him to inquire if all was well. She valiantly replied all was well but caught Elisha by the feet when she came to him, in spite of Gehazi's protests. She refused to leave him until Elisha rose and followed her. Gehazi passed on before them and laid his master's staff on the child's face but came back wearing a long face. The child had not awakened. By the time Elisha came into the house, the child lay dead.

The Shunammite woman waited while Elisha went in, lay upon the child, with his mouth on the child's mouth, his eyes on his eyes, and his hands on his hands. The child's flesh grew warm. Elisha repeated the process. From outside the chamber, the woman heard a sneeze. Another, and another, seven in all. Her heart leaped within her breast. Surely her child lived! Elisha called her in. She beheld her son, then fell at the prophet's feet and bowed to the ground. The son granted by God's mercy had been spared.

THE ISRAELITE MAID

2 KINGS 5

Why do you weep, my mistress?" a little captive maid of Israel, handmaiden in the house of Naaman, captain of the host of the king of Syria, timidly asked. Although she often longed for her own people, she had learned to love Naaman and his wife. He was a great man with the king and honorable. By him the Lord had given deliverance unto Syria. He was also a mighty man in valor and kindly to those who served him.

Now the little maid's mistress lay sobbing as if her heart would break. Again the girl asked, "Why do you weep?"

"Leprosy has come upon Naaman," his wife stammered.

Leprosy! Dreaded and feared by all. And yet—the little maid's heart beat high. She spoke quickly. "Would God my lord were with the prophet that is in Samaria! for he would recover him of his leprosy."

The suffering woman raised dazed eyes to her maid, a feeble hope springing to her face. They scarcely noticed that one who overheard hastily left the chamber. The man repeated word for word what the little maid had said.

Naaman could scarcely believe it, yet anything was better than watching the awful sickness creep over him. He told the king of all Syria, who immediately sent him with a letter to the king of Israel, asking that he heal Naaman.

The Israelite king rent his clothes. He was no God; neither had he the power to cure leprosy.

Mistress and maid waited, hoped, and prayed. Day after day passed. Their hearts sang when Naaman returned unto them. Not a trace of the terrible disease remained. The little maid stood near her mistress while he told his story.

"The king could do nothing, but a man named Elisha said for me to go to him. I came with my horses and chariot and stood by the door of his house." A rueful look went over his face. "Elisha didn't even come outside. He sent a messenger telling me to go wash in the Jordan seven times and my flesh would come again to me and I would be clean."

The little maid's eyes rounded. Her mistress gasped. "How strange! Did he not know who you were?" she disbelievingly asked.

"He had given his command," her husband told her. "I was wroth but still thought he would come forth, call on the name of the Lord his God, and strike the leprosy from my body. If I must wash in a river, why the Jordan? Are not the rivers of Damascus better? When he did not come, I went away in a rage."

"But you are healed!" his wife protested.

Naaman's voice softened. Wonder came into his eyes. "Ah, my brave servants came near and said, 'My father, if the prophet had bid thee do some great thing, wouldest thou not have done it? how much rather then, when he saith to thee, Wash and be clean?'

"I hearkened unto them. I dipped myself in the Jordan. Once, twice, until I rose from the water six times. The leprosy remained." His face took on a look of awe. "The seventh time I rose straightway out of the water clean and purified! This time when I went to the prophet's house, he came out. I said to him, 'There is no God in all the earth, but in Israel.' "

The little Israelite maid clapped her hands in joy. Many times she wondered, was it for this she had been taken into captivity? To be the instrument by which Naaman would find Elisha and be healed? The thought comforted her, and she continued to serve those who never tired of expressing appreciation that she had told them about the prophet of the true and living God.

HEZEKIAH

2 KINGS 18:1–20:21

The Old Testament grimly testifies that Israel had its share of bad rulers. A refreshing exception was Hezekiah. His reign began around 710 B.C. when he was twenty-five years old. Hezekiah "did that which was right in the sight of the Lord." He was completely faithful. No other king before or after him was his peer in this regard. In return the Lord blessed him and helped him prevail against the enemies of Israel.

Hezekiah's greatest challenge came early in his reign when Assyria invaded Judah. "Don't listen to Hezekiah," the Assyrian commander told the frightened Israelites. "His God won't protect you. No other kingdoms have been able to withstand our might. Surrender to us, and live in peace." The Jews began to believe him and to doubt the wisdom and ability of their devout leader.

Hezekiah turned to the great prophet Isaiah for counsel, and Isaiah reassured him that the Lord had doomed the Assyrian invasion to confusion and failure. So it proved. King Sennacherib of Assyria returned to Ninevah and ultimately was murdered by his own sons.

King Hezekiah became deathly ill to the point that even Isaiah predicted he would die. But Hezekiah prayed; the Lord heard and sent Isaiah to announce that the king would live another fifteen years.

Though godly and faithful, Hezekiah did not always make wise decisions. While Hezekiah was sick, the king of Babylonia sent messengers bearing a gift. Gratified by this display of kindness, Hezekiah gave the Babylonian envoys a detailed tour of his country's storehouses and armaments. In fact, there was no strategic secret in all of Judah that Hezekiah didn't imprudently reveal to these seemingly friendly visitors. God told Hezekiah through Isaiah that the result of his carelessness would be the Babylonian conquest of Judah. This occurred a century later.

Hezekiah ruled for twenty-nine years. He was succeeded by his twelve-year-old son Manasseh, who shunned his father's righteous ways and returned to the idol worship Hezekiah had denounced.

EZRA AND NEHEMIAH

EZRA 7:1–10:17; NEHEMIAH

E zra and Nehemiah emerged during a pivotal time in Jewish history. After decades of captivity in Babylon, they led many people back to Judah to rebuild Jerusalem and her temple both structurally and spiritually.

Ezra, a priest and scholar versed in God's law, was a descendant of Aaron, the first high priest. He was in charge of some of the returning exiles. A wonderfully devout man, Ezra led his flock in prayer and fasting. His role was to end the practice of Jews marrying non-Jews from neighboring countries and to return the people to God's ordained pattern of worship.

Meanwhile Nehemiah was still living in Persia where he served as the emperor's wine steward. Nehemiah learned of the difficulties the Jews were encountering in Jerusalem. They lived in fear of surrounding nations, and the protective wall around Jerusalem was in ruins. The Persian emperor granted him permission to go to Jerusalem and supervise the rebuilding of the city's wall. In fact, God so stirred the emperor's heart that Nehemiah was given an escort and building materials.

As the Israelites worked on the wall, their enemies plotted against them. God repeatedly thwarted these plots. Nehemiah prayed often and calmed his people's fears by organizing the workers: Half of them, fully armed, stood guard while the other half toiled at the wall. Even the wall builders carried swords.

When the wall was finished, it was obvious to both the Israelites and their enemies that God's hand had been upon its building. The people asked Ezra to read the law to them, then they prayed, confessed their sins and the sins of their ancestors, and signed an agreement to live in obedience to God.

God's work is often fraught with danger and uncertainty. During the period of the restoration of Jerusalem, the Israelites could not rest easy. Their leaders had to be alert and live in close contact with God. Ezra and Nehemiah rose to this demand.

HADASSAH

ESTHER 1–10

Hadassah, also known as Esther, "the star," had neither father nor mother but dwelt in the house of her cousin Mordecai, who treated her as a daughter. They were of the captive nation of Judah and living in Persia. One day Mordecai said, "The king has sent a decree throughout the land. All wives are to give honor to their husbands. Queen Vashti refused to come at the king's command when his heart was merry with much wine. She has been banished."

Esther felt a tiny pulse beat in her throat.

"All the fair young virgins are to be gathered unto Shushan the palace, to the house of the women. The maiden which pleaseth the king shall be queen instead of Vashti. Esther, think what it would mean should you be chosen."

A flush went over the beautiful face. As queen, she could help her people.

"Do not tell the king you are Jewish," Mordecai warned.

After twelve months of purification rites, Esther went to the king. She so found favor with him that Ahasuerus loved Esther above all the women. He set the royal crown on her head and made her queen instead of Vashti.

Mordecai, who often stood outside the palace gate to hear news of his cousin, learned that two of the king's chamberlains who kept the door planned to lay hands on Ahasuerus. He told Esther, who informed the king. The culprits were hanged and the deed written in the king's chronicles.

Haman, a courtier set above all the princes of the kingdom, hated Mordecai. The Jew would not bow to him. Haman told lies to the king about the Jews and convinced him that the Jewish men, women, and children should be destroyed on a certain day.

Mordecai donned sackcloth and ashes. When Esther sent to know why, he told her of the king's command. He warned that even she could not escape. She sent back and asked all Jews to fast for her.

On the third day, she went and stood in the court. God grant the king would extend his scepter to her. If he did not, she could die for daring to approach him. The king summoned her forward.

Esther invited both him and Haman to a banquet. Once they were there, she made a petition, inviting them to a second banquet the next day. That night the king, unable to sleep, read his chronicles and discovered the service Mordecai had done for him. He also realized Mordecai had never received a reward. The next day, he asked Haman what honor a loyal man should receive. Haman named great things, thinking it would all be for him—then had to see it all bestowed on Mordecai.

At the second banquet that night, Esther courageously exposed Haman's plot. She confessed that she also was Jewish and subject to the decree.

The king immediately hanged Haman on a gallows he had constructed for Mordecai and gave Mordecai Haman's house and his own royal ring. Yet he had no power to reverse the order he had given concerning the slaughter of the Jews, for it had been written and sealed with the king's ring. All he could do was grant the Jews in every part of the land permission to defend themselves.

This he did. He also sent Mordecai out from his presence arrayed in royal apparel and with a great crown of gold. The Jews rejoiced.

No enemy could withstand the fierce fighting of the Jews, once given a decree to defend themselves. Fair and lovely Esther's bravery saved not only her life but the lives of her people. Her story stands today as an example of one who fearlessly took chances and did all she could to right the wrongs done her people, even when her actions could have led to her own death.

JOB

JOB

"Y ou have the patience of Job."

Smile if someone pays you that compliment because Job was one of the most honorable characters in the Bible. He was a wealthy man whose family, fortune, health, and friendships were suddenly taken from him for no apparent reason. Yet he refused to succumb to unbelief. Though he languished aloud, Job knew his Lord had a reason for his predicament, and he patiently waited for things to be made right.

Job lived in the land of Uz and was a faithful believer in God. In fact, God told Satan that Job was the most faithful man in the world.

"The only reason he worships You," Satan retorted, "is that You protect him and bless everything he does. How do You think he would behave if You let him lose all he has? He'll curse You."

"We'll see," God said and let Job's wonderful world collapse around him.

Afterwards Job was visited by three friends, Eliphaz, Bildad, and Zophar. They came to comfort him, but they were hardly a comfort to this godly man. They did not understand Job's devout faith. It seemed apparent to them that Job was being punished because he had done something wrong.

Job knew better. He was not perfect, but he certainly had not committed enough sins to warrant the intensity of sufferings he had been given. Although he demanded to know why God had let him fall into such a state and even became very angry with God, Job never lost faith.

God's reply was a stern and eloquent reminder of His incredible power and the insignificance of human understanding. Job apologized for questioning the Lord's decisions. Then God turned His reproach on the three friends for misinterpreting the meaning of Job's plight. In the end, God made Job twice as wealthy as before.

When we see good people around us afflicted with terrible diseases, tragedies, and setbacks, we should remember Job who lost everything but his understanding of God's faithfulness.

THE IDEAL WOMAN

PROVERBS 31

In a male-dominated world where only the most outstanding (or notorious!) women received much attention, Solomon offers a glowing portrait of the ideal woman. His tribute also elevates everyday tasks and describes the value of those who strive to live up to their God-given womanhood.

Although written to those who lived long ago, much of Proverbs 31:10–31 remains applicable today. The New International Version of the Bible aptly titles this section of Scripture "The Wife of Noble Character."

> A wife of noble character, who can find?
>> She is worth far more than rubies.
> Her husband has full confidence in her
>> and lacks nothing of value.
> She brings him good, not harm,
>> all the days of her life.
> She selects wool and flax
>> and works with eager hands.
> She is like the merchant ships,
>> bringing her food from afar.
> She gets up while it is still dark;
>> she provides food for her family
>> and portions for her servant girls.
> She considers a field and buys it;
>> out of her earnings she plants a
>> vineyard.
> She sets about her work vigorously;
>> her arms are strong for her tasks.
> She sees that her trading is profitable,
>> and her lamp does not go out at night.
> In her hand she holds the distaff

and grasps the spindle with her fingers.
She opens her arms to the poor
    and extends her hands to the needy.
When it snows, she has no fear for her household;
    for all of them are clothed in scarlet.
She makes coverings for her bed;
    she is clothed in fine linen and purple.
Her husband is respected at the city gate, where
    he takes his seat among the elders of the land.
She makes linen garments and sells them,
    and supplies the merchants with sashes.
She is clothed with strength and dignity;
    she can laugh at the days to come.
She speaks with wisdom,
    and faithful instruction is on her tongue.
She watches over the affairs of her household
    and does not eat the bread of idleness.
Her children arise and call her blessed;
    her husband also, and he praises her:
"Many women do noble things,
    but you surpass them all."
Charm is deceptive, and beauty is fleeting, but
    a woman who fears the Lord is to be praised.
Give her the reward she has earned, and let
    her works bring her praise at the city gate.

ISAIAH

ISAIAH

Isaiah is one of the best-known Hebrew prophets. He spoke for God in Jerusalem during the eighth century B.C. at the time when Assyria conquered Israel and carried many victims into exile.

According to Isaiah's own description, he was a Jew "of unclean lips" living in an unclean nation. In a vision he saw the Lord sitting on a throne attended by winged seraphs. One of the seraphs took a live coal from the Lord's altar, flew down, and touched Isaiah's lips with the coal. "Now your record has been blotted clean, and you no longer are guilty," the angel told him.

The Lord needed a spokesman to show the Israelites their sins and turn them back to His ways. "Whom shall I send?" God asked.

"Here I am," responded the awestruck Isaiah. "Send me."

Isaiah prophesied for forty years during the reigns of four kings. He knew the Israelites had much more to fear from their own wrongdoing and lack of faith than they did from the Assyrians. He preached to Israel before and after their captivity. He reminded them of God's faithfulness to their ancestors and taught them that God is in control of all history.

"Do you think I have divorced you like a man divorces his wife?" God asked the downtrodden Israelites through His prophet. "Then where are the divorce papers?" God still loved His people, Isaiah proclaimed, and would rescue them. He said that the Lord was building a new creation, a place of peace, where there would be no sorrow or death. "Therefore rejoice!" Isaiah exhorted.

Throughout his prophecies, Isaiah foretells the coming of the Messiah, a descendant of Jesse, a cornerstone, shepherd, and bearer of salvation. With good reason Isaiah cried, "Rejoice!"

JEREMIAH

If you think you're too young or too ordinary to be used by God, consider Jeremiah. He was probably still in his teens when God called him to prophesy in Judah. Jeremiah thought he was too young and not a particularly good speaker. But the Lord would have none of these protests. "Go where I tell you to go," God commanded. "Do not be afraid; I'll be with you." He touched Jeremiah's mouth and told him, "I have put My words in your mouth."

The Lord sent Jeremiah to Jerusalem where the prophet delivered God's indictment to the sinful, idolatrous people. He pointed out their unfaithfulness and that of their ancestors. He asked them to return to God. He repeatedly warned of invasion from the north: Jerusalem was about to be devastated. Jeremiah went so far as to tell the Israelites to surrender to the Babylonians rather than die in battle.

The people were not happy to hear this message, especially coming from one so young. But Jeremiah also preached that the Lord would rescue the Israelites and rebuild their nation after they returned to Him. But that did not mollify the people's anger. The Jews plotted to kill Jeremiah and actually threw him in prison for his preaching.

More than any other prophet, Jeremiah revealed his own disgruntlement and questions. "You told us we would have peace, but a sword is at our throats," he whined to God. He personally agonized as he told the people of their coming defeat. When they laughed at him, he expressed his anger openly.

Perhaps because of his youth, Jeremiah held nothing back. But he was mature spiritually. This is seen in his prayer, "I know we humans are not in control. Punish me as I deserve—but not in anger, for that would kill me." Jeremiah reminds us that God is in control of every situation.

EZEKIEL

D em bones, dem bones, dem dry bones. . .
    Dem bones gonna rise again. . . ."
Apart from the African-American spirituals we have sung for generations, most Christians have only a sketchy acquaintance with the prophet Ezekiel.

Ezekiel prophesied in the sixth century B.C., just before Jerusalem's fall and as the Jews were exiled into Babylon. He had a singular encounter with the Lord who showed him an astounding vision: Four living creatures, each with four faces, and four wings, appeared within a shining windstorm; each creature had four faces, one of a human, a lion, a bull, and an eagle; beside each creature was a bright wheel within a wheel with eyes around the rims. At length Ezekiel realized he was witnessing a form of the Lord's glory. In this way God appointed Ezekiel to prophesy to the Israelites.

Early in his book, Ezekiel warned the people of Judah that their sins would bring about the ruination of Jerusalem. He predicted the captivity of the Jews and urged the people to return to the Lord's ways. Ultimately he described Jerusalem as a worthless vine that needed to be punished and put to shame. He also predicted God's judgment against rival nations: Ammon, Moab, Edom, Philistia, Tyre, and Egypt.

A most memorable part of Ezekiel's prophecy is his vision of the nation of Israel as dry bones lying in a valley. God promised that He would free these dead, hopeless bones from their entombment and cause them to live again.

Ezekiel foretold the restoration of Jerusalem and described in detail how the temple would be rebuilt. He explained the way worship would be conducted in that new temple and how the land would be subdivided among the Israelites upon their return. His prophecy covers the concerns of the captive people with warnings, encouragement, and assurances that they would in time regain their lost kingdom.

DANIEL

DANIEL

From the time of his youth, it was obvious Daniel was to be used by the Lord for important work. Then the Babylonians captured Jerusalem. Still, Daniel and three of his friends were outstanding among the Hebrew captives because of their youth, intelligence, handsome appearance, and strength. Therefore, they were selected to be trained for service in King Nebuchadnezzar's court.

But Daniel—who had been given the Babylonian name Belteshazzar—demonstrated his determination to live in the godly way in which he had been raised, even if it meant jeopardizing his favored standing among his captors. Nebuchadnezzar ordered that the trainees be given royal food and drink, thinking it would maximize their strength and wit as they grew. But the food was unacceptable according to Jewish custom. Daniel asked his guard to give him and his three friends only vegetables and water.

"What if you end up looking paler than the other trainees?" the guard said. "Then I'll be killed for disobeying the king's orders."

"Try it for ten days," Daniel suggested. "Then compare us with the other boys."

Not only did they pass the test; their austere, clean diet made them fatter and healthier than the others.

After three years of training, all the young men were interviewed by King Nebuchadnezzar. Daniel and his three friends far surpassed the others in every skill. So the king appointed them to important court positions and relied on their wisdom when he needed advice.

Daniel was particularly wise and had the God-given power to interpret dreams, as well. This earned him the king's deepest respect; Daniel was made a governor and named chief counselor. But Daniel made it clear that his abilities did not imply he was in any way superior to any of the other advisors. Rather, he said, God simply had chosen to use him to explain certain things.

Daniel and his friends—whom the Babylonians had named Shadrach, Meshach, and Abednego—were faithful to God in the face of their captor's idol worship. On one occasion, Shadrach, Meshach, and Abednego were thrown into a furnace for refusing to worship a towering gold statue erected near the city. The heat of the furnace was so intense that it killed the men who guarded it while its intended victims, accompanied by an angel, walked unhurt in the fire. King Nebuchadnezzar was so impressed that he had to respect their God. In time, he himself came to believe in God.

Daniel served under Nebuchadnezzar, his son Belshazzar, King Darius, and later King Cyrus of Persia, and won the highest respect of each of them. It was Belshazzar who commanded that Daniel interpret the mysterious handwriting that appeared on the wall of the king's banquet hall. The message, Daniel accurately interpreted, foretold the end of Belshazzar's reign.

During Darius's reign, governors and officials who were jealous of Daniel's wisdom and power contrived to have the king issue a decree forbidding anyone in the kingdom to pray to any god—on pain of death! Naturally Daniel continued to pray daily. This was reported to Darius. He was horrified because to uphold his decree he would have to order the execution of Daniel, his most trusted advisor. Reluctantly, he had Daniel cast into a den of lions and then prayed himself that God would save his servant.

And God did so by sending an angel to keep the lions at bay throughout the night. In the morning, Darius ordered Daniel released and his accusers thrown to the lions. Then the king ordered everyone in his kingdom to worship Daniel's God, whom Darius recognized as the one true God.

AN ISRAELITE MOTHER

DANIEL 1–3, 6

Many times, far more can be learned about a woman's life from the actions of her children than what is recorded concerning her personally. Such is the case of four Israelite women, especially Daniel's mother. The light of her calling to motherhood shines steady and bright through the life of her son.

Nebuchadnezzar, king of Babylon, sat on his throne and pondered. Suppose he tried an experiment. His clever mind turned a growing idea over and over, then he called his chief court official to him. "Bring me children of Israel who are of royalty. They must have no blemish, but be well favored, wise and cunning. They must understand science and have ability to stand in the king's palace and learn our language." A curious smile brightened his face. "We shall see what comes to pass."

All that he commanded was done. Young men, carefully selected, were transplanted from their native land to Babylon. For three years they would have a daily portion of the king's meat and of the wine he drank. So nourished, they would then stand before the king.

Among the Israelites were Daniel and three who became Shadrach, Meshach, and Abednego. How did their mothers feel, seeing the sons they had borne and nursed taken away to a land of heathen customs? Surely many prayers went with the young men. Picture a parting scene between Daniel and his mother:

"My son, forget not all thy father and mother have taught thee. Forsake not Jehovah, the one true God."

Daniel bows his head. "I shall forget neither thee nor thy teachings."

"Peace be unto you," the mother brokenly tells him.

"And to you." He walks away, then turns, raises one hand in farewell, and disappears from the home he loves. From henceforth, his dwelling shall be among strangers.

A niggling worry attacks the watching mother. She cries out in a voice so low only God can hear. "Lord God of Israel, hear my plea. Has this, thy servant, prepared her son to face what lies ahead?" She shivers, imagining a hundred unknown dangers. "I cannot go with him, Lord. I cannot cradle his tired head against my bosom or soothe him in times of perplexity. Only Thou, O God, can make him strong." She strains tear-dimmed eyes, but her son is gone.

The courts of Babylon are like nothing the young Israelite men know. Daniel clings to the fact he has found favor with the chief official, who has been set over him, Shadrach, Meshach, and Abednego. He sees sympathy in the man's eyes. That and their mothers' teachings give him and his companions the courage to stand the first of many hard tests.

"Why do you refuse the king's meat and not drink of his wine?" the anxious official demands. "The king will have my head should you look worse than the other young men."

They explain such eating and drinking would defile them. From childhood, they have eaten pulse (vegetables) and drunk water. Daniel proposes that for a time they be given only pulse and water. At the end of ten days, they will compare their health with that of the others. The official agrees. To his amazement, all four stand strong, straight, and none of the others are like unto them.

Test after test comes. Yet always the knowledge of praying mothers and the early teachings so important to the young Israelites' development into manhood serve them well. By the power of God revealed in a night vision, Daniel interprets a dream King Nebuchadnezzar cannot even remember how to tell. He and his faithful friends refuse to worship the king. God closes lions' mouths and sends One to walk with the children of Israel in the fiery furnace so not one hair on their heads is singed. The kingdom marvels. In uprightness of heart, those men—brought up in the fear of the Lord by godly mothers—despise heathen gods and ways. They cling to their early teachings and glorify Jehovah in word and deed.

NEBUCHADNEZZAR

DANIEL 1–4

I t took a lot of convincing for King Nebuchadnezzar of Babylon to decide to worship God. He reigned during the sixth and seventh centuries B.C. at the time Jerusalem was captured. Daniel and his colleagues, carried into captivity by the Babylonian army, were trained for royal service. In time, they were given important managerial positions under Nebuchadnezzar. Daniel, in particular, became indispensable to the king because he was able to interpret Nebuchadnezzar's strange dreams. The king respected Daniel and the others, but he gave little thought to their God.

When Shadrach, Meshach, and Abednego refused to worship Nebuchadnezzar's golden idol, he had them thrown into a fiery furnace. They survived and emerged unsinged, as if nothing had happened. The king was amazed and promoted them to more powerful positions, but still he declined to worship their God.

But the Lord in His kindness reached out to Nebuchadnezzar. As He often does, God used affliction to draw the king to Him. God took away Nebuchadnezzar's kingdom and power for seven years. Nebuchadnezzar later described himself as living like a wild animal during that time. Some students of Scripture believe this was a result of an hallucination or mental derangement. Whatever the condition, Nebuchadnezzar at last prayed to Daniel's God. He was healed and restored to power.

Nebuchadnezzar gave this testimony of praise: "Glorify the King in heaven, for He is truthful and fair, and He humiliates the proud." Clearly, God had struck a nerve in Nebuchadnezzar when He demonstrated that He was Lord even over that which matters most to a king—his royal pride.

HOSEA

The unfaithful wife deserted her husband for a lover. The husband paid her return to his household! This, the story of the prophet Hosea, parallels the message he brought to the people of Israel. Israel had betrayed their Lord like a promiscuous wife, yet God in His mercy was willing to buy them back!

Hosea could understand the agonizing relationship between God and His wayward people better than any other prophet because he knew similar agony in his own life. He could speak to the Israelites bluntly and harshly but with genuine underlying love. He knew of the pain they were causing their Maker by their long history of disobedience. And God's pain was heightened by the fact that He loved them passionately.

Hosea's prophecy contained a straightforward accusation against the people's sins and idolatry. "Judgment is coming," he warned. "Bondage will follow. You have trusted in your own power so you will reap destruction."

But near the end of his book, Hosea poignantly conveyed God's irrevocable love for His people. "How can I give you up?" God said. "I am not man, I am God, and I love you tenderly. I will not vent My wrath on you." Hosea concludes with a plea that Israel repent, and a final assurance of God's forgiveness if the people would only turn back to Him.

JOEL

JOEL

L ocusts! The plague that swept through Israel around the fifth century B.C. was one of the most dramatic in Old Testament history. God used it to punish His sinful people and through the prophet Joel promised His forgiveness if they changed their ways.

Joel likened the locusts to a hostile army, a nation, and "a people great and strong." Far too many to be counted, the locusts were laying waste the land of Israel which once had been as fruitful as the Garden of Eden. These locusts got Israel's attention, and then Joel sounded the alarm. Hopefully the Israelites would listen to his warning of judgment day.

Joel prophesied that when Israel repented, God would bless them again by sending His Holy Spirit. Their enemies would be punished, and the faithful would be saved. He spoke of the day of judgment when the sun would be darkened, the moon turned to blood, and enemy nations would lie desolate. But God's people would find refuge in a land where the mountains "drop down with sweet wine" and the hills "flow with milk."

Joel's is a prophecy of stark contrasts—light and darkness, good and evil, struggles in punishment and rest in God's presence.

Amos

AMOS

The Lord roars out of Zion. . . ."
    So begins the prophecy of Amos, a sheep breeder and keeper of fig trees in Tekoa, a town in the land of Judah. God told him to leave this work and preach to the people of Bethel in Israel. Amos obeyed.

His message was indeed a roar. Amos began by proclaiming the Lord's judgment against the neighboring nations of Syria, Philistia, Phoenicia, Edom, Ammon, Moab, and Judah. He then declared God's wrath against Israel for a long litany of offenses. Amos particularly cited the rich who mistreated the poor and those who worshipped lifeless idols.

"Return to Me and you will live," he told the Israelites. Amos promised a coming day of doom but concluded with the Lord's pledge to rebuild the fallen kingdom.

Amos is among the twelve minor prophets of the Old Testament and was the first biblical writer to teach that God rules the entire universe.

JONAH

JONAH

Storms on the Mediterranean Sea can be fearful, and none was more ominous than the one that boiled there in 862 B.C. and engulfed a little ship outbound from Joppa.

The vessel rocked dangerously and was deluged by wave after great wave while the crew tossed cargo overboard to lighten the load. They also prayed fervently. But the storm intensified.

They thought that perhaps someone among them had provoked the Lord's wrath and brought on this calamity. Then they remembered the passenger Jonah. They knew he was fleeing from God. Yet he was fast asleep despite the drastic pitching of the vessel. Who was he? What had he done to bring on such terror?

Jonah admitted he was the likely cause of their peril. And he told the crew the solution—throw him into the sea, then the waters would calm. The sailors at first could not bring themselves to do this. They tried to maneuver the ship toward land, but it was futile. So they followed Jonah's brazen advice and cast him into the sea. Immediately the storm abated.

Jonah was a Hebrew prophet. The Lord had commanded that he travel to Nineveh, a huge city on the river Tigris far to the northeast of Judea. There he was to warn the people that their wickedness would soon be punished. It seemed to Jonah that this was a long way to go for nothing but trouble. So he fled by ship in the opposite direction. Jonah wanted the Lord to find another prophet for his difficult and dangerous mission to Nineveh.

Despite Jonah's attempt to flee from God, his disobedience was used for God's purposes. The experience of the storm and the sudden calming of the waves was such a dramatic demonstration of the Lord's power and grace that the crew of the ship worshipped God and pledged to honor Him.

Meanwhile, God had no intention of letting Jonah off the hook—even by death. So a gigantic fish swallowed the hapless man after he was cast from the ship. For three days the fish swam the sea with Jonah alive in its belly. The wretched prophet prayed for his life and repented, and the Lord heard. At God's command, the leviathan vomited Jonah onto the shore.

Jonah followed God's orders, journeyed to Nineveh, and preached to the people that, because of their sinfulness, their city would be destroyed in forty days. The people listened, stopped their evil ways, and asked the Lord's forgiveness. The Lord forgave them and granted their city a reprieve from judgment.

However, instead of being overjoyed at the Ninevites' change of heart, Jonah was angry. God sent him on this exhausting, dangerous errand, knowing full well that in the end the people would repent and be forgiven! "I want to die," the pitiful Jonah told the Lord. "You care about the wrong things," said the Lord. "It is right for Me to be concerned for a great city like Nineveh."

ZECHARIAH

ZECHARIAH; MATTHEW 26:31

Rejoice, Jerusalem!
Shout, Jerusalem!
Your King is coming.
He is righteous, and He brings salvation.
He is gentle, and He rides on the foal of a donkey. . .

Thus Zechariah predicted the coming of Jesus Christ, more than five hundred years before His birth. The Jews had returned from captivity in Babylon and began rebuilding the temple and the city of Jerusalem. Zechariah spoke not only of their labors in Jerusalem but of things to come as well. These include the punishment of Israel's ungodly leaders and of the nation's enemies, the coming of the Messiah, the people's repentance from their idolatrous ways, the Lord's final victory over His enemies, and the millennial kingdom.

Jesus Himself referred to Zechariah's prophecy during the Last Supper. "Tonight," He told His disciples, "all of you will stumble because of Me." Then He quoted Zechariah: "Kill the Shepherd and the sheep will scatter."

Zechariah's prophecies serve as stern, necessary warnings to wayward people. They are also words of hope, and vital connectors from Old Testament history to Jesus Christ, and to the building of His glorious Church.

MATTHEW

MATTHEW; MARK 2:13–17; 3:13–19;
LUKE 5:27–32; 6:12–16; ACTS 1:12–14

A Jewish tax collector was not a desirable companion in first-century Palestine where the Jews lived under bondage to Roman taxes. Yet Matthew was called by Jesus and joined His band of disciples. When the Pharisees demanded to know why Jesus associated with "sinners and tax collectors," Jesus replied, "Those who are well do not need a doctor. I've come to call sinners, not righteous people, to repent."

Matthew wrote an in-depth account of Jesus' life and teachings. Whereas Luke wanted to reach Gentile readers with the good news of Jesus' salvation, Matthew's objective was to convince Jews that Jesus was the Messiah as foretold in the Old Testament.

Matthew's record provides the most thorough version of the Sermon on the Mount. He emphasized Jesus' concern with righteousness and concluded with the commission Jesus gave the disciples just before He ascended into heaven: "Go, make disciples in all the nations. . ."

Little is known of Matthew's life. Varying accounts say he died in Ethiopia or Macedonia, possibly of natural causes, possibly by execution.

MARY, THE MOTHER OF JESUS

MATTHEW 1; LUKE 1–2

Clip-clopping hooves of a little donkey chosen more for strength than beauty sent spirals up from the dusty road two travelers plodded. Mary shifted in a vain attempt to find a more comfortable position. "I pray we shall reach Bethlehem soon," she told the sturdy man who walked beside her.

"It is not far now," he encouraged. A slight frown wrinkled his sweaty forehead. "Is it well with thee and thy babe?" He anxiously glanced at her cumbersome body, great with child.

"It is well." She smiled at her husband and smothered a small, secret sigh. The journey from Nazareth had been long and hard. Swarms of people crowded the roads and made traveling difficult. Rich and poor, in health and sickness, old and young, all sought their birthplace to be counted and taxed, for the decree of Caesar Augustus exempted no one.

The little donkey plodded on, one ear drooping. Mary rested against the rolled blankets Joseph had thoughtfully strapped on the donkey and the strong hand he placed against her back. Weariness swept over her like waves on the Sea of Galilee, blurring the present, recalling the past. . .

Mary slowly opened her eyes. Had someone called? Nay. Quiet lay over the room like a shimmering veil. And yet—

"Hail, thou that art highly favored, the Lord is with thee: Blessed art thou among women." A glowing figure stood beside her.

Mary shrank in terror. What manner of salutation might this be?

The angel—for such he must be—said, "Fear not, Mary: For thou hast found favor with God. And, behold, thou shalt conceive in thy womb, and bring forth a son, and shalt call His name JESUS. He shall be great and shall be called the Son of the Highest: And the Lord God shall give unto Him the throne of His father David:

And He shall reign over the house of Jacob for ever; and of His kingdom there shall be no end."

She, bear a child? Although she was espoused to Joseph the carpenter, they had not yet become man and wife. "How shall this be, seeing I know not a man?" Mary asked, unable to tear her gaze from the shining figure.

The angel replied, "The Holy Ghost shall come upon thee, and the power of the Highest shall overshadow thee: Therefore also that holy thing which shall be born of thee shall be called the Son of God." He went on to tell her, "Behold, thy cousin Elisabeth, she hath also conceived a son in her old age: And this is the sixth month with her, who was called barren. For with God nothing shall be impossible." Truth radiated in every word.

Belief and acceptance stirred in Mary's heart. The Lord God of Israel who created the earth and the heavens, who parted the sea and fed His children in the wilderness, possessed power that knew no bounds. "Behold the handmaid of the Lord; be it unto me according to thy word," Mary whispered. Joy and trembling filled her soul, and she bowed in humility. When she raised her head, the angel had departed from her.

After a time of pondering all the things the angel had said, Mary knew what she must do. "I will arise and go to Elisabeth," she decided. So began a time of newness for the Jewish maiden. Her visit with Elisabeth confirmed the truth of all she had been told, yet a great wall rose in Mary's life. Could Joseph, loving and kind as he was, believe what had come upon her? Or would he think her a bad woman, one who sought to cover her sins with wild tales.

In fear and trembling, Mary related all the angel had said. She saw the shock in Joseph's eyes, the pain and disappointment that one he had thought pure should come to this sad state. Should he make her a public example, she would be stoned. What, then, would become of the babe she carried, the child the angel said was the Son of God?

A just man who loved Mary with all his heart, Joseph considered the matter day and night. He was minded to put her away privily, for he could not bear to see her stoned, even if she had sinned against heaven and against him.

While he thought on these things, the angel of the Lord appeared unto him in a dream. "Joseph. . .fear not to take unto thee Mary thy wife: For that which is conceived in her is of the Holy Ghost."

The angel spoke other things, confirming Mary's story, then departed. Joseph raised from his sleep. He wanted to climb to the rooftops and shout to any who might listen, "She is innocent! My Mary is pure and chosen among all women to bear a son who shall be called Emmanuel, 'God with us.' " When he told Mary all that had come to pass, they rejoiced together.

In the months that followed, Mary found herself in a strange state. She hugged knowledge to her heart and marveled. Sometimes her heart beat until she thought it might burst. Why had she, of all the virgins in Nazareth, nay, in the entire land, been chosen to bear the Son of God? She thought of other maidens, older and more experienced than she, worthy and devoted. Would she be able to succor and care for the child in the proper way? Yet each time doubts came, the razor-sharp memory of the angel's visit, the words that had burned into her heart, rose to reassure her. And each time, she bowed herself and humbly prayed she might be worthy of the great honor and responsibility to which she had been called. . .

"Mary." A gentle hand pressed her shoulder. She returned from her remembrances. "We have reached Bethlehem."

A sharp pain tore through her. "It is a good thing," she gasped and laced her fingers together over her swollen belly.

"Hasten, little friend," Joseph told the donkey who obligingly broke into a faster pace. Yet as the three travelers went from inn to inn and found no place, Mary fought ever increasing pain. At last a kindly innkeeper offered them a place in a dry, warm cave where he kept his animals. By then Mary little cared for anything except a place to rest and deliver her child. What mattered it whether he be born in inn or stable? She must have shelter and soon.

Before the cock crowed, Mary brought forth her firstborn son. She wrapped him in swaddling clothes and laid him in a manger. Spent, she held him close, sensing the present moment might be the most precious of her life. A little later, she roused to voices. Shepherds knelt before her, faces working, eyes turned toward the babe. They told her angels had proclaimed the baby's birth while they were in the fields keeping their sheep. They glorified God and praised Him. Mary tucked their visit away in her heart to be pondered later.

From glory to agony, from childbearing through Jesus' childhood to the cross and beyond, Mary, mother of Jesus, is history's finest reminder that with God, nothing shall be impossible.

JOSEPH, THE HUSBAND OF MARY

MATTHEW 1–2; LUKE 1:26–56; 2:1–50

Joseph of Nazareth learned that Mary, his betrothed, was expecting a child! He knew this was not his child, so naturally he decided to divorce her, though privately so as not to expose her to public disgrace. But in a dream, an angel told Joseph that Mary's baby was conceived by the Holy Spirit and would grow to become the Savior of the world.

So Joseph married Mary. But during the pregnancy, the couple had to travel to Bethlehem in Judea and register their names as part of a census ordered by Augustus Caesar. There was played out the well-known story of the king born in a stable. Joseph named the infant Jesus, as he had been instructed to do. Then he was warned by an angel that Herod the Great was looking for the baby Messiah. So Joseph fled with his family to Egypt where they stayed until Herod died and it was safe for them to return to Nazareth.

Joseph must have wondered how this normal little child could grow to become the Messiah! But when Jesus was twelve Joseph caught a glimpse of Jesus' greatness. As usual, the family went to Jerusalem to celebrate the annual Passover feast. Afterward, on the way home among the throngs of other pilgrims, Mary and Joseph noticed Jesus was not with them. Worried, they turned and hurried back to Jerusalem. There they found Jesus in the temple, of all places, carrying on intelligent discourse with the scholarly teachers!

"Why are You here?" they demanded. "We've been looking everywhere for You."

"Don't you know I need to be here, in My Father's house?" He replied.

But He returned home with them and grew up an obedient boy.

Joseph of Nazareth was given a very special role in history. He struggled as an ordinary father and husband to provide for his family in a captive society. Yet he was the father chosen to provide protection and nurture to the Son of man.

JESUS CHRIST

For the prophets He is the Messiah.
For Mary He is a son.
For God He is the Son.
For Herod He is a threat.
For the wise men He is the King of the Jews.
For the shepherds He is heralded by angels.
For Simeon He is the consolation of Israel.
For the religious leaders He is a challenger.
For His fellow Nazarenes He is an outcast.
For the demon-possessed He is the liberator.
For the blind He is the giver of sight.
For the lame He is the transformer.
For the dead He is the reviver.
For the hungry multitude He is the provider.
For the children He is the defender.
For sinners He is forgiveness.
For the ignorant He is the teacher.
For the storm-tossed He walks on water.
For the diseased He is the healer.
For lost sheep He is the shepherd.
For the sins of the world He is the Lamb of God.
For Thomas He is an enigma.
For Judas Iscariot He is a profit source.
For Pontius Pilate He is an annoyance.
For witnesses of the Crucifixion He is contemptuous.
And for all who receive Him, who believe in His name,
He gives power to become children of God.

How could the people of the first century believe that the Messiah had at long last arrived? Jesus Christ was certainly not what they expected. He did not act like a king, or even a priest. He selected commoners, even sinners, for companions and loved the poor, the rich, the young, the old, the Jew, the Gentile, the persecutor, and the persecuted. There was no one He did not love.

There is no one Jesus Christ does not love. He receives all who come to Him and can be reached instantly by anyone from anywhere. One can never intrude upon Jesus. He waits to hear from you!

JOHN THE BAPTIST

MATTHEW 3; 4:12; 11:2–19; MARK 1:1–11; 6:14–29;
LUKE 1; 3:1–22; 9:7–9; JOHN 1:19–37

P repare the way of the Lord!"
This was the task of John the Baptist, son of Zacharias and
Elisabeth. He was a powerful preacher in the Judean desert who
wore camel skin clothes and ate a diet of locusts and wild honey.
People came to John in great numbers, and he admonished them to
repent and confess their sins, whereupon he baptized them in the
river Jordan. Was he the Messiah? they asked. No, he replied. But
soon the Messiah would appear and would baptize not with water
but with the Holy Spirit.

One day John's cousin Jesus came to be baptized. This, John
knew, was the man whose arrival he had predicted. "You should baptize me instead," John protested.

But Jesus reassured him. "This is the way God wants us to do it."

So John baptized Jesus in the river. When the Lord emerged
from the water, the Holy Spirit came down from the sky and descended upon Jesus like a dove. A voice from heaven proclaimed,
"This is My beloved Son. I am well pleased with Him." Thus began
Jesus' ministry.

Shortly afterward John was thrown into prison by King Herod.
This occurred because Herodias, Herod's wife, was angry that John
had denounced their marriage. She had previously been Herod's
brother's wife, and John told Herod that he was wrong to take his
brother's wife. Herodias wanted John killed, but Herod, who feared
John's popularity, preserved the prophet's life and merely imprisoned him.

John was unsettled by doubt while in prison and sent this message to Jesus, "Are You really the Messiah?"

"Tell John what you are seeing and hearing," Jesus told John's
disciples. "The blind see, the lame walk, those with leprosy are
healed, the deaf hear, the dead are raised up, and the poor receive the

news of salvation. God will bless those who do not reject Me."

This reassurance came at a critical time because Herodias soon found a way to end John's life. Herodias's daughter danced for Herod and his guests at a birthday celebration. The king was so captivated by this that in a moment of weakness he promised her anything she desired. Prompted by her mother, the girl demanded, "Bring me the head of John the Baptist."

Herod was shocked and distraught, but he could not go back on his promise. So the great John the Baptist, forerunner of Jesus Christ, was beheaded to appease a sinful queen.

John's epitaph is Jesus' own words: "What did you go out into the desert to see? . . .a man dressed in fine clothes? No, those who wear fine clothes are in kings' palaces. Then what did you go out to see? A prophet? Yes, I tell you, and more than a prophet. . . . Among those born of women there has not risen anyone greater than John the Baptist."

John the Apostle

Matthew 4:21–22; Mark 1:9–20; 10:35–45;
the Gospel of John; Acts 3:1–4:31; 8:14–17;
1, 2, and 3 John; Revelation

John and his brother James followed in the footsteps of their father, Zebedee, and became fishermen. Their friends, the brothers Andrew and Peter, were also fishermen. All four were called to be His disciples by Christ early in His ministry.

In the Gospel, John gave us firsthand accounts of many of the Savior's miracles, beginning with the wedding at Cana where Jesus turned the water into wine, all the way to Jesus' visitations after His resurrection. Although John did not record all the miracles he saw, he offered ample proof that Jesus is the Son of God.

John's Gospel makes effective use of metaphor: In it Jesus is a Shepherd to His flock, the Living Bread and the Water of Life, the Light of the World, and the True Vine. John was a brilliant thinker, an eloquent writer, and passionate in his devotion to the Savior. So much so that from the cross Jesus asked him to care for His mother.

After Jesus' ascension, John labored among the churches in Asia Minor and is credited with writing Revelation and the Epistles of John. Historians believe that of the original twelve disciples only John died a natural death in his old age.

PETER

MATTHEW; MARK; LUKE; JOHN;
ACTS 1–5, 9–12; 1 PETER; 2 PETER

S imon Peter was introduced to Jesus Christ by his brother Andrew. Jesus told the brawny fisherman, "You will be named Cephas," a name which means "a stone."

Peter was involved in one of the Savior's first miracles. Jesus had been preaching from Peter's fishing boat to the multitudes gathered along the shore of the Sea of Galilee. When He finished speaking, Jesus told Peter to row into deep water and let down his fishing nets.

"But there are no fish here," Peter complained wearily. "We've been fishing all night, and we've caught nothing."

But he did as Jesus suggested—and caught so many fish that his nets started breaking. His partners came to help, and they pulled up so many fish their boats started to sink.

Awestruck by Jesus' power, Peter fell at His feet. "Stay away from me," Peter told Him. "I'm a terrible sinner."

Jesus already knew this, and it did not affect His plans for Peter. "I'm going to make you a fisher of men," Jesus told him. After Jesus' resurrection and ascension, Peter was leader of the early church. He was a simple, seemingly impulsive man who did not consider the consequences of his words and deeds.

Peter must have been shaken to his sandals when at the Last Supper Jesus said, "Simon, Satan has asked to sift you like wheat. I have prayed that you will remain faithful." Peter could not imagine what perils Jesus referred to, but he was confident that he would follow the Lord anywhere. "I am even ready to die with You," Peter promised. Jesus corrected him. "Before the rooster crows in the morning, you will deny Me three times."

When Jesus was arrested in the garden, Peter tried to defend Him and struck one of the assailants with his sword, cutting off an ear. Jesus admonished Peter to put away his weapon and with a touch healed the wounded man. Shortly afterward, Jesus was taken into custody in a house. Peter stayed outside warming himself around a fire. A servant girl asked, "Weren't you one of His followers?"

"I do not know Him," Peter replied impulsively, fearing for his own safety. Twice more during the next hour, Peter was openly suspected of following Jesus. Both times Peter repeated his denial.

It's sad that the triple denial comes to mind when Peter's name is mentioned because Peter truly became a stone built into the spiritual house which is the Church of God.

A WOMAN
OF FAITH

MATTHEW 9; MARK 5; LUKE 8

S he knelt before Jesus in fear and trembling, an insignificant woman in the midst of a multitude. Desperation and fear had driven her to seek the new prophet, whose wonders were being whispered, shouted, and sung throughout her land. At first she had scoffed. Was not Jesus the son of a Nazarene carpenter?

"Yea," those who spoke to her confirmed. "Yet He is much more."

She considered well whether to present herself to this man of whom she knew nothing except gossip. Would it not be better to go on without hope than to allow herself to believe the teacher might have a cure for the rare blood disease that had plagued her for twelve endless years?

Physician after physician had examined her, sadly shaken their heads, and said they could do nothing. Each time, she died a little more inside. Why such a thing had come upon her, she knew not. Apathy often caused her to ask, "Does it matter? Soon I must die, and that will be the end."

Memories of a time before the illness destroyed her dreams danced before her. Oh, to once again run free and well through the fields. To walk without weakness, straighten to full height, and move without pain. *It cannot happen if you do not keep seeking a cure,* a voice whispered in her heart.

One evening when she lay sleepless, the woman decided. "I will arise in the morning and seek this Jesus. I will cast myself at His feet. If He is all people say, He will have mercy on me. If not, I die and the pain will be no more." She knew it would require her last measure of strength to travel the short distance to Jesus.

In spite of her determination, in spite of her belief that Jesus was her last and only hope, the stricken woman's heart quailed at the sight of the throng surrounding the One she sought. She felt weakness wash through her as waves washed against the shore during a storm. She could go no farther.

A slight opening in the crowd gave her a glimpse of Jesus. It was enough to renew her. *If I may but touch His garment, I shall be whole,* she said in her heart. She stretched forth her hand. The edge of Jesus' cloak felt rough against her searching fingers. Strength flowed into her. She opened her mouth to cry out she had been healed, but no words came.

Jesus, immediately knowing that virtue had gone out of Him, turned and said, "Who touched My clothes?"

His disciples replied, "Thou seest the multitude thronging Thee, and sayest Thou, who touched Me?"

But Jesus looked round about to see her that had done this thing.

She knelt before Him in fear and trembling. "Lord, it was I. I knew if I could but touch the hem of Your garment, I would be healed." Head bowed, she waited. What would He do?

Jesus spoke, in a voice like unto none she had ever before heard. "Daughter, be of good comfort; thy faith hath made thee whole."

Her faith? Words hung on her shaking lips, the confession of how little faith she had possessed. She looked into Jesus' face, filled with compassion and understanding that swept away any need for explanations.

Tears rained like skies weeping for an unbelieving world. She again bowed her face to the ground, only vaguely aware when the multitude moved on—some following Jesus to ask for blessing; others out of curiosity. Then she stood, praised God, and ran, rejoicing with each breath of air that filled her lungs, every long stride that carried her on her way.

Jairus's Daughter

Jairus loved his daughter with a love known only to those who have been blessed with one child. When she was stricken with illness, he nearly went mad with grief. She must not die, this child whose twelve short years had blessed his household mightily.

"I will seek out Jesus, of Nazareth," he said. "If all the tales of Him are true, He will surely heal my child."

When he reached Jesus, the crowd made way. Was not Jairus one of the rulers of the synagogue? Jairus fell at Jesus' feet, worshipped, and besought Him greatly, saying, "My little daughter lieth at the point of death: I pray Thee, come and lay Thy hands on her, that she may be healed; and she shall live."

Jesus arose and followed Jairus, as did His disciples.

On the way, a disturbance came in the crowd. Jairus seethed with impatience. To one in his daughter's condition, every moment mattered. Why must a tottering woman slow them? The next moment he caught his breath. The woman who barely grazed the hem of Jesus' garment with her fingertips was made whole! Jairus's heart leaped within him. If the Master could heal with only that slight touch, how much more would He do when He laid hands on the child who lay just outside the gates of death?

Jairus's heart sang then turned to stone when some of his own household rushed out saying, "Thy daughter is dead: Why troublest thou the Master any further?" An unworthy thought crept into his mind and took lodging. Why had Jesus tarried to heal the woman and allowed a child to die? Was the woman's life of more importance than the maiden's?

Did Jesus perceive his thoughts? Perhaps, for He spoke. "Fear not: believe only, and she shall be made whole."

Jairus stumbled on, torn between the assurance in Jesus' eyes and the utter impossibility of the dead being restored to life. When they at last reached Jairus's home, Jesus permitted only Peter, James,

John, Jairus, and his wife to come into the chamber. All the rest wept and bewailed, and when Jesus said, "Weep not; she is not dead, but sleepeth," they laughed Him to scorn.

Jesus ordered them all out. He took the maiden by the hand and called, saying, "Maid, arise."

Her spirit came again, and she arose straightway: And Jesus commanded her parents to give her meat.

Jairus felt faint with astonishment and joy. He saw from his wife's face that she felt the same. When they attempted to thank Jesus, He charged them they should tell no man what was done. But the fame of Jesus' raising Jairus's daughter went abroad into all that land.

PHILIP

MATTHEW 10:1–4; MARK 3:13–19; LUKE 6:12–16;
JOHN 1:43–51; 6:5–7; 12:20–22; 14:8–14

One of the first evangelists on record was the apostle Philip. Soon after he was called by Jesus, he told the skeptic Nathaniel, "We've found the one Moses and the prophets were writing about! He's Jesus of Nazareth."

"Can anything good come out of Nazareth?" Nathaniel grumbled.

There must have been a twinkle in Philip's eye when he replied, "Come and see."

And Nathaniel followed the Lord.

Before miraculously feeding the five thousand at the Sea of Galilee, Jesus likewise must have had a twinkle in His eye when He turned to Philip and asked, "Where can we get enough bread for all these people to eat?"

Philip shook his head in dismay. "Six months' pay wouldn't buy even a sampling for this many people."

Jesus took all the available food—five loaves of bread and a couple of fish—and turned it into a feast.

Still Philip needed reminding. At the Last Supper, Jesus told His disciples, "No one can come to the Father except through Me."

"Lord, show us the Father," Philip requested. "Then we'll be convinced of what You say."

"Philip, have I been with you all this time, and you still do not know Me?" Jesus answered. "Believe that I am in the Father, and the Father in Me. If you cannot believe My words, then believe because of the miracles you have seen Me perform."

Philip did believe and helped spread the gospel after Jesus' resurrection and ascension. He is thought to have been martyred in Asia Minor.

JUDAS ISCARIOT

The other apostles never dreamed one of Jesus' twelve closest followers would conspire to turn Him over to His enemies to be falsely accused, tried, and executed.

Judas Iscariot was chosen by Jesus along with the other apostles to go out and preach for Him. He also served as the disciples' treasurer. But he seems to have placed an emphasis on money rather than devotion. When Mary poured perfume upon the Lord, Judas criticized her. "This perfume should have been sold and the money given to the poor," he said. But Jesus respected Mary's gesture and corrected Judas. "The poor will always be with you," Jesus said, "but I will not always be with you."

At the Last Supper, Jesus predicted that one of the twelve who were eating with Him would betray Him. "Surely it can't be me!" cried Judas, although he already had bargained secretly to turn Jesus over to the chief priests for thirty pieces of silver.

"You have said so," Jesus replied.

Later that night, when Jesus went to pray in the Garden of Gethsemane, Judas appeared with a mob. "Rabbi!" greeted Judas, and kissed his master. The word *Rabbi* was the code which Judas would use by arrangement to identify Jesus in the darkness.

The mob dragged Jesus away to be tried. But soon Judas heard that Jesus had been given the death sentence. He sorely regretted his betrayal and so took the thirty pieces of silver back to the priests and told them that he had sinned. "Jesus is innocent!" he said. When they refused to listen, Judas threw the money into the temple, went out, and hanged himself.

By law, the priests could not put Judas's silver in their treasury—it was blood money. Instead they used it to buy land for a graveyard where nameless strangers could be buried.

Thomas

MATTHEW 10:1–4; MARK 3:13–19;
LUKE 6:12–16; JOHN 11:14–16; 14:1–7;
20:24–29; ACTS 1:12–14

Thomas seems to have been a wet blanket over the joy Jesus spread throughout the land.

When Jesus announced to His disciples they must go to Bethany where their friend Lazarus had just died, Thomas remarked sarcastically, "Yes, let's all go there and die." At the Last Supper, Jesus assured His apostles He was going to prepare a place for them in the Father's house, and they knew the way to follow Him there. Thomas challenged, "How can we know the way, since we don't even know where You are going?"

And in the aftermath of the Crucifixion, when Jesus appeared to His followers, Thomas did not believe their reports of seeing the Master. He would not believe, he vowed, unless he could actually touch the nail-scarred palms and put his hand in the Lord's wounded side. Later Jesus entered the locked room where the disciples were staying, and He showed Thomas the pierced hands and had him feel the wound.

"My Lord and my God!" Thomas cried.

"You believe because you have seen Me," Jesus said. "Blessed are those who believe without seeing."

Thomas joined his colleagues in spreading the good news. Yet still today a skeptic is called a doubting Thomas. But Thomas is an important example to us. All the objective evidence in the world could not convince Thomas that Jesus Christ had risen from the dead. It wasn't enough to be told of the Resurrection—not even by his most trusted friends. Thomas had to see Jesus for himself. He had to have a personal encounter with the Savior. And so it has always been for Christ's believers.

JAMES, THE BROTHER OF JESUS

MATTHEW 13:55; MARK 6:3;
ACTS 12:17; 15:12–21; 21:18; GALATIANS 1:19

I magine growing up the brother of Jesus Christ and not knowing that He was the promised Messiah until after the Crucifixion and Ascension.

James knew how Jesus liked His eggs cooked; how He reacted after hitting His thumb with a hammer; how He handled incidents of sibling banter and rivalry; His favorite games. As James grew up with Jesus he did not know that his brother was the incarnate God. Years later he surely remembered the incidents of Jesus' childhood, adolescence, and young manhood with a different understanding.

Some scholars think that James did not become a believer until after Jesus' death and resurrection. Details of his life are few, and learning about him is difficult because the New Testament records four men by the name of James. After Jesus' resurrection, was it His brother James who became head of the first-century church in Jerusalem? Was he the writer of the New Testament letter bearing his name? Some scholars suspect so; others are not sure.

Regardless, envision yourself as Jesus' own brother!

HEROD ANTIPAS

MATTHEW 14:1–12; MARK 6:14–29;
LUKE 23:7–12

Unscrupulous yet cautious, Herod Antipas ruled Galilee during the lifetime of Jesus Christ. His father, Herod the Great, had been completely heartless when he ordered the cold-blooded killing of every baby boy around Bethlehem in an attempt to eliminate the newborn king of the Jews. Like his father, the younger Herod had no love for Jesus or for John the Baptist. Their ministries were causing an unprecedented sensation throughout the land, but Herod Antipas was not as ruthless as his father. In fact he tried to avoid the conflict which these men would cause him.

Yet Herod Antipas had a particular disdain for John. Herod had taken his brother Philip's wife as his own and John had boldly pointed out his wrongdoing. The king wanted to arrest and execute John for this, but he was afraid the people would revolt because of their high regard for John.

Then the wife in question, Herodias, forced Herod's hand. She persuaded Herod to have John arrested. Then, using her daughter's sensual dancing to corrupt his thinking, Herodias obtained an order to have John beheaded. This unnerved the ruler. Not only did he fear the people's reaction, he privately appreciated John's preaching. But he had promised to do whatever his pretty niece wanted, and at her mother's request, she asked that John be beheaded and his head presented to her on a platter. So it was done.

When Jesus Christ was arrested and dragged before Pilate in Jerusalem, Herod happened to be in the city. Pilate tried to take advantage of this in an effort to shift the role of judge to Herod Antipas. So Pilate sent Jesus and His accusers to Herod. After all, Jesus was a Galilean, so His case came under Herod's authority. Herod was eager to meet Jesus because he wanted Him to perform a miracle. But Jesus refused to answer Herod's questions. So Herod and his soldiers mocked the prisoner and sent Him back to Pilate.

Scripture says Herod and Pilate, who had been enemies, became friends in the aftermath of Jesus' crucifixion. These two cowardly leaders found a common bond at the turning point of civilization. They may have feared this man from Galilee, but they could not acknowledge the existence of a power above their own or that of Rome.

HERODIAS

MATTHEW 14; MARK 6

Many were those Herodias, ex-wife of Philip, now married to Philip's brother, hated. Her legendary rages effectively quelled opposition for fear of the retribution she mercilessly dealt out to any who dared speak against her. Yet of all her foes, none loomed larger in her twisted mind than John, the Baptizer.

Each time Herodias thought of the wild prophet who had come from the wilderness to thunder and stir up the people, she gnashed her teeth in fury. "How dare he speak against us?" she demanded of Herod, her brother-in-law and husband. "If you do not care that he cries in the streets that you are breaking the law, what about me? Should not the tetrarch have the right to take whatever woman he desires, whether or not she be married to his brother?" She clenched her hands with their painted nails until they became claws, working as if she had her enemy's throat between them and would throttle out John's life.

"Be still," Herod commanded. "You know how powerful John has grown. The multitude who believe in him and count him a prophet daily grows larger." He hesitated and spread his hands in a helpless gesture. "Is it not enough that I had him bound and thrown into prison?"

"Pah! It will never be enough," she retorted. "He has insulted and attempted to shame us before all the people. He must pay with his life. You should have had him executed long since."

"I tell you, I cannot," Herod roared.

Herodias only sneered, secretly despising him for his weakness. If she had the power to order John's death, she would have done so the moment he dared raise his voice and condemn those he should bow down and worship. "Are you then afraid of him?"

"Nay," Herod lied. "But the Baptizer is a just man and holy." He did not add that he had observed John, even heard him gladly, until the prophet publicly denounced him for his adultery.

Herodias said no more at the time. Yet with each passing day, she hated John more and vowed to do him harm in whatever way she could.

Plot after plot came to mind. She would know no peace until John's body lay in the ground and his impudent tongue was forever silenced. Even from his cell, he continued to cry out against her and Herod for their illicit relationship.

Herodias brazenly kept the silken curtains of her litter open when carried through the city streets. She stared into the faces of those she passed, and her wrath against John increased. For although Herod's subjects bowed low in obeisance, their scornful expressions and the epithets hurled at her from the security of the multitude brought flags of scarlet to her vapid, painted face.

"I will bide my time," she vowed. "Then I will strike." Again she curled her sharp-nailed fingers into claws, and anticipation spread over her like honey warmed in the sun.

SALOME

MATTHEW 14; MARK 6

S alome clasped her hands in delight. "I am really to dance before the court?"

Herodias smiled a curious smile. "Yes, my pet. You must dance as you have never danced before. Much is at stake."

Salome failed to catch any particular significance in her mother's voice. To dance before Herod was great enough honor. To be chosen to perform at the great feast the tetrarch had ordered in honor of his birthday overwhelmed her. Some of her confidence fled. "What if I do not please him?"

Herodias eyed her daughter's beauty, her slim and graceful figure. A gleam came to her calculating gaze. "You shall please him." She tossed her head and laughed. "Herod and the lords, high captains and chief estates of Galilee will be so drunken with wine a damsel with far less charms than you could entertain them. You must do much more, Salome. You are to dance in a way not seen in the court, one that entices and drives men mad at the sight of you. Do you hear?"

A deep flush rose in the girl's smooth cheeks. An uncanny resemblance to the mother who demanded adulation as her due showed in her countenance. "I hear and obey." She half-closed her eyes, already planning how she could be more daring, more seductive than all those who had preceded her in Herod's court.

On the great day, Herodias carefully ordered her daughter to remain secluded until time for her dance. She watched and waited, a jeweled spider decked out in royal raiment. Wine flowed like the Jordan in spring. Now came the moment for which Herodias waited. She dared not prolong Salome's entrance much longer or Herod would be too drunk to fully appreciate the young girl's ravishing dance.

"Now," she beckoned.

Salome burst upon the court in the most sensual dance ever

performed. She saw men's eyes widen with lust for her barely concealed body. She saw Herod's hot gaze fasten itself on her and danced on, until he called her to him. "Ask of me whatsoever thou wilt, and I will give it thee." He held his cup for more wine and swore, "Whatsoever thou shalt ask of me, I will give it to thee, unto the half of my kingdom!"

Salome's eyes glistened. Half the kingdom, for her? She opened her mouth to speak, to request jewels, riches beyond belief. Nay, first she must consult with her mother. Much wiser in the ways of the world, Herodias would advise her daughter well.

"What shall I ask?" she demanded of Herodias.

"The head of John the Baptizer."

Salome recoiled. Her eyes widened. Her breath came in labored gasps.

"Do as I tell you," Herodias commanded. "For your sake as well as mine. Should the people take it into their heads to stone me, you will not be spared. The Baptizer must be silenced if we are to live." Triumph gleamed in her eyes.

Terrified at the threat, Salome straightway hurried back to the king. "I will that thou give me here in a charger the head of John the Baptizer."

Silence fell over the court. The shock in Herod's eyes showed Salome's demand had partially sobered him. Regret clouded his face, and he opened his mouth, glanced around the gathered guests, and halted. Salome followed his thoughts. He might be willing to give the other half of his kingdom to undo his rash promise, but he would not. To do so would make him an object of contempt.

Herod gave the command. Soon after, the executioner returned. For a moment Salome stared at the platter. She drove her teeth into her lip to keep down nausea. She closed her ears against the horrid sounds of retching by those sober enough to care. In silence so heavy it hung like a shroud, Salome turned, fixed her gaze straight ahead, and carried her gruesome burden to an ecstatic Herodias.

No one knows if Salome ever wept bitter tears or was haunted by nightmares for her evil deed. History only records she danced, and John paid with his life for daring to speak out against evil wherever he found it, even in the highest places.

THE CANAANITE WOMAN

MATTHEW 15; MARK 7

For many years a woman of Canaan cared for her daughter. Grievously vexed with a devil, the girl writhed and threw herself back and forth, wailing and gnashing her teeth until her mother thought she would die. Sometimes her secret heart wished she would. Death could surely be no worse than life as the maiden lived it.

Why had they been so cursed? All who dwelt on the coasts of Tyre and Sidon knew their story and shunned them. How long must a mother watch the one she had given life being destroyed by a devil?

"There is a Jew called Jesus who travels in the land," a neighbor told the distraught woman after the worst spell her daughter had ever suffered. She lowered her voice, as if afraid to be overheard. "It is said He heals those who come to Him."

The mother laughed bitterly. "A Jew heal the daughter of a woman of Canaan? Such a thing could not be!" Yet as the attacks increased, she knew she must pursue every rumor on behalf of her daughter.

When the woman came to Jesus, she immediately began to cry in a loud voice, "Have mercy on me, O Lord, Thou son of David; my daughter is grievously vexed with a devil," then held her breath waiting for His reply.

Jesus answered not.

She cried again.

The disciples, impatient with her pleadings, besought Jesus, "Send her away; for she crieth after us."

But He answered and said, "I am not sent but unto the lost sheep of the house of Israel."

The woman's hope flickered like a lamp with only a few drops of oil. Should she leave off beseeching Him? Nay. Better to risk the wrath of the One she implored than go away heavy-hearted. She fell at Jesus' feet and worshipped Him, saying, "Lord, help me."

Jesus answered and said, "It is not meet to take the children's bread, and to cast it to dogs."

Goaded by her great need, the woman refused to be silent. She refused to let Jesus walk away, for if He did, all hope must go with Him. "Truth, Lord: Yet the dogs eat of the crumbs which fall from their masters' table."

She dared not look up, dared not risk looking at Jesus or the disciples who indignantly murmured against her that she should speak so to the Master.

Then Jesus answered and said unto her, "O woman, great is thy faith; be it unto thee even as thou wilt." And her daughter was made whole from that very hour.

The woman of Canaan is a permanent reminder how love and concern for others and faith born of despair can prevail even when circumstances appear hopeless.

THE TEN VIRGINS

MATTHEW 25

Ten virgins—five wise and five foolish—are characters in a parable Jesus told. A parable is "an earthly story with a heavenly meaning."

"Good friends, our lamps are growing dim," a maiden said to her companions. "We must go forth, buy oil, and fill them lest they go out before the bridegroom cometh." She reached for shawl and veil.

Four of the nine virgins she addressed straightway rose up. They went with her into the marketplace and purchased oil to replenish their supply.

"Why do you make haste?" the other five wanted to know. "It is yet day. The bridegroom tarries. There is plenty of time to fill our lamps before he comes." They chattered and laughed together, poking fun at the five virgins industriously filling and polishing their lamps until they shone brightly.

The hour grew late, and the household became weary, but no word came from the expected guest. At last, all retired and fell into deep slumber.

At the midnight hour, a great cry sounded throughout the streets of the city. "Behold, the bridegroom cometh; go ye out to meet him."

The ten virgins immediately arose and joyously trimmed their lamps. The five who had failed to fill their lamps cried, "Give us of your oil; for our lamps are gone out."

The others shook their heads. "Not so; lest there be not enough for us and you: But go ye rather to them that sell, and buy for yourselves."

The five foolish virgins who had whiled away their time in mocking their wiser sisters wasted no more time. They rushed into the marketplace, pounded on an oil merchant's door, and clamored for him to open his shop, that they might purchase oil.

The door remained shuttered; the shop dark and bare.

"We must have oil," the frightened girls told one another. "We will try another merchant."

While their companions were out attempting to buy oil, the bridegroom came. Great was the joy of the five virgins who were ready and waiting for him. They went in with him to the marriage, and the door was shut behind them.

From dark street to dark street the foolish five ran, beating on doors, trying to rouse anyone who might sell or lend them oil for their empty lamps. They railed against their five wise sisters, saying they should have shared their oil. Yet they knew in their hearts if the situation was reversed, they would not dare give away precious oil and risk not having enough for themselves.

What little oil remained in their lamps had long since vanished. Heavy of heart, the five virgins turned toward home, hoping for some miracle to fill their lamps that they might be found ready to be admitted to the marriage feast.

At last they reached the house. The door stood firmly shut. All their trying could not open it. "Lord, Lord," they implored. "Open to us."

But He answered and said, "Verily I say unto you, I know you not."

Five foolish virgins huddled together in outer darkness, weeping bitterly at having lost their chance simply because they had not prepared during the time given to make ready.

Historians say a faithfully observed custom in those days was the setting of the marriage time by the bridegroom. He chose any day within a two-week period and made ready, then sent a messenger to announce his arrival. All ten virgins surely knew the custom. Five prepared ahead of time. The other five acted on the premise there was no hurry, with dire results—offering a lesson well worth heeding.

PONTIUS PILATE

MATTHEW 27:1–2, 11–31; MARK 15:1–20;
LUKE 3:1; 23:1–25; JOHN 18:28–19:22

Pontius Pilate was the Roman governor of Palestine in the time of Christ. The last thing he wanted to deal with was some explosively sensitive, incomprehensible altercation among the Jews in Jerusalem. But he was charged with hearing and judging local disputes.

One such dispute raged between the Jewish leaders and Jesus of Nazareth. Jesus was arrested and dragged before Pilate early one morning. Pilate heard the case and questioned Jesus. He was very surprised that Jesus did not respond to the accusations of the chief priests and elders of the Jewish people. He could find nothing that Jesus had done wrong. When Pilate learned that Jesus was a Galilean, he tried to defer judgment to King Herod who happened to be in Jerusalem at the time. But Herod and his men merely beat and mocked Jesus and sent Him back to Pilate.

Pilate had a diplomatic way out of this mess. He had a custom of releasing a prisoner at the time of the Jewish Passover each year and had in custody a particularly troublesome criminal named Barabbas. "I can give you Barabbas, or I can give you Jesus," Pilate told the people gathered at Jesus' trial. He hoped the crowd would pick Jesus to be released. Then he would not have to deal with the chief priests' claim. But the mob had been stirred up by the Jewish elders. They picked the dreadful Barabbas to be set free.

Pilate's wife had had a very disturbing dream about Jesus. "Have nothing to do with that man," she warned. But Pilate had to do his duty. He asked the mob again whether they wanted him to release Jesus or the criminal Barabbas. "Give us Barabbas!" they demanded. So Pilate washed his hands in front of everyone, meaning that he considered himself free from blame if the innocent man was executed. "Kill Him yourselves," he told the Jewish leaders.

To Pilate, the judgment of Jesus Christ was a harrying

annoyance. It may have been a dramatic incident, but at the time he basically regarded his role in one of the most important events in the history of civilization as little more than a distraction from his routine duties.

PILATE'S WIFE

MATTHEW 27

First, restlessness. Then, dreams without form or substance, more terrifying than any the wife of Pontius Pilate, the governor of Judea, had ever known. "No. No!" A scream burst from her throat and tore the fabric of sleep to shreds. She bolted upright and threw back the silken bed coverings that threatened to smother her.

"Mistress, what is it?" Maidens in her service ran to the chamber, eyes enormous in their white faces.

Slowly, the hard beating of her heart stilled enough for her to whisper, "Where is my husband?" Perception sharpened by the dream that yet clutched at her with frightening fingers, she caught their hesitation and quick exchange of glances.

"Answer me," she ordered, with an imperious gesture.

"Even at this moment he questions a prisoner," one faltered.

"The man called Jesus?"

"Yea."

She sank back against her cushions and waved them away, feeling the blood drain from her face. Jesus, who haunted her dreams until she felt she would go mad. The distraught woman pressed her hands to her aching temples. Why had Pontius Pilate ever consented to accept the post of procurator here in this miserable land? Her lip curled. Enemies in high places were surely responsible for the ignominious assignment. Ever since they arrived, there had been nothing but trouble. In his ignorance of those he had been sent to rule, Pilate had made one mistake after another and incurred the hatred and wrath of his subjects.

"I cannot think of it," the tormented woman cried. Yet how could she not think of it? The entire land of Judea rang with gossip concerning the man who now stood in the judgment hall before her husband.

"Just another rabble-rousing Jew," Pontius had said when told the chief priests and elders took counsel against Jesus to put Him to death. Yet in spite of his bold statement, he shifted uneasily. "I don't like this. They bring their squabbles to me when they should be solving them. What good are they if they cannot settle their own disputes?"

"It is more than that," his wife pointed out. "This Jesus has spoken out against the Pharisees and scribes, calling them corrupt, whited sepulchers."

"Perhaps He should be praised rather than condemned." Pilate smiled sardonically. "That bunch of hypocrites is no more qualified to lead than the swine they despise." He sighed. "What must be will be. They have no authority to give an execution order."

"So they come to you," she bitterly told him.

"Yea." He strode out, leaving her to ponder.

Now the wife of Pilate slid from her couch and clapped her hands. When her maidens came running, she ordered them to bring her writing materials and hastily wrote:

"Have thou nothing to do with that just man: For I have suffered many things this day in a dream because of Him."

"See this is taken to the governor at once," she commanded, then paced the floor of her luxurious rooms a long, weary time—until slow, heavy steps announced the coming of her husband. Before he entered, she could tell things had not gone well.

"I washed my hands of it," he mumbled. "I told the multitude I was innocent of the blood of the just man. They said, 'His blood be on us, and on our children.'" He stared at his shaking hands, called for a pitcher and water, and washed his hands again.

She said nothing. Pontius continued in a voice so dead it brought shivers to her body. Misery shone in his dull eyes. "I found no fault in Him, but what could I do? They said I was no friend of Caesar if I released Jesus. It is over."

Nay, his wife's heart shouted. *Your misery—and mine—is only beginning.*

MARY MAGDALENE

MATTHEW 27; MARK 15–16; JOHN 20

Mary Magdalene, out of whom Jesus had cast seven devils, writhed with pain. The Master had done so much for her. Why could she not have done more for Him? Although she, along with a few other women, had followed Jesus and ministered to Him, all they could do was stand helplessly by and watch Him die on the cross between two thieves.

She and Mary the mother of Joses had sat near the sepulcher, silently grieving. When they went home, the Sabbath passed slowly. How could life continue? Mary thought of herself before Jesus healed her, of the spells that came over her without warning and turned her into a madwoman. All it had taken to free her was a single touch. She could still feel the warmth that flowed through her, healing her spiritually and cleansing her of all sin.

At last the Sabbath passed. On the first day of the week, at the rising of the sun, Mary Magdalene joined Mary the mother of James and a friend named Salome. Carrying sweet spices to anoint Jesus' body, they came to the sepulcher. "Who shall roll away the stone from the door of the sepulcher that we may enter?" one asked. The women looked at one another in dismay. After Jesus died and was taken from the cross, Joseph of Arimathaea, an honorable counselor who also waited for the kingdom of God, had boldly gone to Pilate and asked for the body of Jesus. The governor agreed. Joseph brought fine linen, took Jesus down, and wrapped Him. He laid Jesus in a sepulcher hewn out of rock. A great stone was rolled up to the door and guards were set by Pilate. Three women, no matter how determined, would not be able to move the stone.

"Behold!" Mary pointed, gasping for breath. "The stone has been rolled away!"

"How—when—where are the guards?"

The entrance to the sepulcher looked wide and empty. The women looked at each other and hesitantly stepped inside. They fell to their knees in fright, for a young man clothed in a long, white garment sat on the right side. His countenance was like lightning, and his raiment white as snow.

"Be not affrighted," he said. "Why seek ye the living among the dead? He is not here but is risen: Remember how He spake unto you when He was yet in Galilee, saying, The Son of man must be delivered into the hands of sinful men and be crucified, and the third day rise again. But go your way, tell His disciples and Peter that He goeth before you into Galilee: There shall ye see Him, as He said unto you."

Marveling, unable to believe what they had seen and heard, the women fled. Mary Magdalene went straight to Simon Peter and John. "They have taken away the Lord out of the sepulcher, and we know not where they have laid Him," she cried. In broken phrases, she told the disciples what the angel had said. Peter and John hastened to the sepulcher, but only the linen clothes and napkin lay as mute evidence one had been there. Unable to understand it, they went to their homes.

Mary could not bear to leave. She stood outside the sepulcher weeping, then bent down and looked in. Two angels in white sat, one at the foot, the other at the head of where Jesus' body had lain. They asked why she wept and she repeated, "Because they have taken away my Lord, and I know not where they have laid Him." Blinded by her tears, she turned and faced a man she supposed to be the gardener.

He said, "Woman, why weepest thou? whom seekest thou?"

She pleaded for Him to tell her where Jesus had been taken, but He said unto her, "Mary."

That voice! Joy flooded her soul. "Rabboni!" ("Master!")

"Touch Me not, for I am not yet ascended to My Father," Jesus said.

Heart pounding, she ran and found the disciples. They believed not, for they had not seen. But Mary of Magdala knew Jesus lived again, even as she lived anew when Jesus cast out the seven devils and made her a new creature in Him.

BARABBAS

G ive us Barabbas!"
The prisoner cringed as he heard the mob outside the Roman governor's house. Had his time come so soon? The famous criminal Barabbas was awaiting execution. His crimes: murder, theft, and insurrection. Dragged before the Roman governor Pilate, Barabbas was outwardly defiant but inwardly terrified. The crowd was screaming for blood—his blood. But wait. Barabbas listened again to the shouting crowd. They did not want his blood; they were demanding his freedom!

Another prisoner was present, bound, beaten, and bleeding. He was Jesus the Nazarene who claimed to be the Messiah. Barabbas had heard of this man and His many miracles. Jesus, they said, healed the sick, confounded the wisdom of the scribes and Pharisees, and even raised the dead to life. Yet there He was, tortured and humiliated. Pilate gestured to Jesus and then to Barabbas and asked the bloodthirsty crowd, "Which of these men do you want me to set free?"

Everyone knew that during the yearly Passover celebration Pilate's custom was to release a prisoner of the people's choosing. On this occasion their choice was between the untainted and the terrorist—Jesus and Barabbas. Barabbas could not believe his ears. Not only had the surging crowd chosen him to live, but he would be set free!

Then Pilate washed his hands as a symbol that he was not responsible for taking Jesus' innocent life. It was the crowd (or the crowd's instigators) who were to bear this liability. He ordered Barabbas released and Jesus scourged.

Barabbas said nothing as he waited impatiently for the guards to unshackle him and did not pause to watch the flogging of the

Nazarene. Fearful that the people would change their minds, Barabbas fled into the morning, retreated to the back streets of Jerusalem, and disappeared from history.

One may ask, did Barabbas ever wonder about the innocent man who had taken his place on the cross that day—the One who died in his place? Did he repent? Did he believe? Or did the reprieved Barabbas continue to live as a criminal? Does he live today in the understanding of New Testament readers as the model of all of humanity—deserving of death but released to life by the sacrifice of God's Son?

MARK

MARK; ACTS 12:12, 25; 13:5, 13; 15:36–39;
COLOSSIANS 4:10–11; 2 TIMOTHY 4:11;
PHILEMON 23–24; 1 PETER 5: 13

The young disciple Mark was eager to spread the wonderful news of Jesus Christ, especially to the non-Jewish world. His Gospel is the shortest of the four and possibly was the first to be written.

Mark's enthusiasm shows in his action-oriented writing. He skips altogether the story of the Savior's birth and begins his account with Jesus' baptism by John the Baptist at the onset of His ministry. By the end of the first chapter of the Gospel of Mark, Jesus has already resisted Satan, chosen four disciples, and performed many miracles of healing and exorcism.

Mark labored with Paul, Peter, Barnabas, and others to build up the early church. It is thought that Mark was martyred like his fellow workers. According to one account, Mark was dragged to death through the streets of Alexandria.

The Poor Widow

Jesus loved to watch people. He yearned over them and longed for them to break the bondage formed by sin and be free. He rejoiced when they listened to Him and laid aside their burdens, prejudices, and hypocrisy. He wept when they turned away—but always, He watched.

One day He sat watching those who came to the treasury and cast in their money. He noticed the careless way the rich flung in much, then went away with heads held high, proud to have done their duty so magnificently. Perhaps He sadly smiled, knowing they had their reward by being seen and noted for their generosity.

A poor widow hung back until the more worthy finished making their offerings, then she timidly came forward. Evidences of poverty showed in her clothing, the workworn hands that had obviously known great toil. Her tired fingers fumbled in her cloak and drew forth two mites, which make a farthing.

For a moment, she stared at the small amount of money, then cast it in with the rest. She disappeared into the crowd, little dreaming her deed would be known until time ran out.

Jesus called unto Him His disciples. He said to them, "Verily I say unto you that this poor widow hath cast more in than all they which have cast into the treasury."

The disciples looked at one another in amazement. How could the two mites, which make a farthing, compare with the golden coins thrown into the treasury by those of great wealth?

Jesus went on to explain. "All they did cast in of their abundance; but she of her want did cast in all that she had, even all her living."

As the widow of Zarephath gave the last of her meal and oil to the prophet Elijah, so the woman in Jesus' time gave everything she had. If she could speak to us down the path from the past, perhaps this devoted servant would tell of blessings as great as those experienced by her giving counterpart who lived hundreds of years earlier.

LUKE

LUKE; ACTS

Which of the four authors of the Gospels was a medical doctor? Whose meticulous, methodical writing style gives him away? It was Luke.

This thorough biblical writer handed down parables and details about Jesus' life that are found nowhere else. For example, Luke sought to convince readers that Jesus Christ came back to life physically after the Crucifixion. To accomplish this, the writer pointed out that the resurrected Savior ate fish with His disciples. This unique bit of evidence emphasizes a physical resurrection.

Luke also wrote the book of Acts as a continuation of his Gospel. It chronicles the spread of Christ's church during the first century. Luke accompanied the apostle Paul through Asia and Macedonia. This book of New Testament history shows how the early Christians struggled not only to spread the gospel but to understand how the gospel applied to their world.

Tradition says that Luke met a martyr's death, hanged on an olive tree in Greece.

ELISABETH

Mary's cousin Elisabeth lived with her husband, Zacharias, in the hill country of Judah. Word of their righteousness spread throughout the land, for they walked blameless in all the commandments and ordinances of the Lord. Yet one thing they lacked: a child. Elisabeth was barren, and both she and Zacharias were aged.

Zacharias served in the priest's office and burned incense in the temple of the Lord. One day an angel appeared and stood on the right side of the altar. Fear fell on the old priest. But the angel said, "Fear not. . .thy prayer is heard: And thy wife, Elisabeth, shall bear thee a son, and thou shalt call his name John."

The angel said John would be great in the Lord's sight, many would rejoice at his birth, and he would be filled with the Holy Ghost even from his mother's womb. But Zacharias could not believe. "Whereby shall I know this? for I am an old man, and my wife well stricken in years."

The angel announced he was Gabriel, sent by God. Because of Zacharias's unbelief, he would be dumb—unable to speak until all had been accomplished.

Elisabeth conceived. Great was the old couple's joy, but the priest remained dumb. Elisabeth sang at her work and dreamed of the day she would deliver her firstborn. How good God was to remove her barren state and thereby take away her reproach among men!

In the sixth month, Mary came to pay Elisabeth a visit. The moment Mary saluted her cousin, Elisabeth felt her babe leap within her. The Holy Ghost loosed her tongue. She blessed Mary and the babe she carried within her. Mary responded with a song of praise.

For three happy months, Mary dwelt with Elisabeth. How they talked, the two who had been chosen to be mothers in Israel: one of the Son of God, the other of one who would turn many hearts toward the Lord. After Mary returned to her home, Elisabeth brought forth a son. Her heart swelled with pride when her neighbors and her cousins heard how the Lord had showed great mercy. They rejoiced with her—but Zacharias remained dumb.

Would he ever speak again, Elisabeth wondered? She contented herself in caring for her son, little heeding those who protested when she said he should be called John.

"There is none of thy kindred called by this name," they protested, when on the eighth day the child was brought for circumcision.

They made signs to Zacharias. He called for writing materials and confirmed the baby should be called John. Immediately his tongue loosed. He praised God and prophesied of that to come.

Elisabeth cherished her son, yet she never forgot the prophecies concerning him. Scripture does not tell whether she lived to see John grow and wax strong in spirit. Did she watch him enter the desert in which he would abide until his time came? Was she one who entered the waters of baptism at his hand? If alive at the time, surely she agonized when an act of wanton wickedness ended his ministry. All that is known is the exemplary life of this godly mother of John the Baptizer who fulfilled her role and rejoiced at having been blessed in her old age.

ANNA

LUKE 2

For fourscore and four years, Anna, the prophetess, departed not from the temple but served God night and day. Once she had been married, but after only seven years, her husband died. Each year of service saw her grow a little older and a little slower. Yet she refused to let the ravages of time force her to leave off her fasting and prayers. What dreams did she dream? What knowledge did she gain during eighty-four years in the temple and well over one hundred years of living? The things she saw in that long time span would surely fill many volumes.

One day Mary and Joseph brought their little son to the temple. Anna watched Simeon, who had been told he would not see death before he had seen the Lord's Christ, take Jesus in his arms and bless Him.

Anna's heartbeat quickened. She crowded closer. "Thanks unto the Lord," she cried. Strength beyond her years filled her. She spoke of the child called Jesus to all who looked for redemption in Israel. Simeon's words echoed in her ears, "Lord, now lettest Thy servant depart in peace, for mine eyes have seen Thy salvation which Thou hast prepared before the face of all people; a light to lighten the Gentiles, and the glory of Thy people Israel." Perhaps Anna's heart echoed Simeon's cry. Once she had seen Jesus' face, what more had life to offer?

A WOMAN
OF THE CITY

LUKE 7

A woman of the city known to be a sinner learned Jesus of Nazareth had consented to eat with Simon, a Pharisee. She considered and planned what she would do. The Master deserved tribute; she had the means to give it to Him.

While they sat at meat, she entered Simon's house, carrying in both hands her most precious possession: an alabaster box of ointment. She stood at Jesus' feet and wept, then washed His feet with her tears. She used her long and lustrous hair to dry them, then kissed the Master's feet and anointed them with ointment.

Simon glared at her. She could read his displeasure in the gaze he turned toward her. To have such as she dare enter his home and minister to Jesus was beyond decency. If He was the prophet people proclaimed, surely He would know her for a sinner and refuse to allow her to touch Him.

Jesus suddenly spoke, addressing his host. "There was a certain creditor which had two debtors: The one owed five hundred pence, and the other fifty. And when they had nothing to pay, he frankly forgave them both. Tell me therefore, which of them will love him most?"

Simon answered, "I suppose that he to whom he forgave most."

Jesus smiled. "Thou hast rightly judged." He turned to the woman, but said unto Simon, "Seest thou this woman? I entered into thine house, thou gavest Me no water for My feet; but she hath washed My feet with tears, and wiped them with the hairs of her head.

"Thou gavest Me no kiss; but this woman since the time I came in hath not ceased to kiss My feet. My head with oil thou didst not anoint, but this woman hath anointed My feet with ointment.

"Wherefore I say unto thee; her sins which are many are

forgiven; for she loved much: But to whom little is forgiven, the same loveth little."

Jesus said unto her, "Thy sins are forgiven."

The woman kneeling at His feet could speak no word. Never since she became notorious had a man spoken to her so. She felt as though she had stepped under a fall of clear water, cleansing and pure.

A quick glance around the circle of watching guests showed their confusion, their inner wonderings of who Jesus could be to forgive sins.

Jesus told her, "Thy faith hath saved thee; go in peace."

Somehow she managed to rise and sedately leave the room, although she longed to leap into the air and cry out with joy. Somehow she made her way down a street that looked far different than when she had trod it on the way to Simon's abode. Jesus' admonition rang in her ears. "Go in peace." Peace! Something she had dreamed about and never thought to find. Now, in a twinkling, it had come.

The alabaster box was empty, but the woman's heart filled to bursting. A new life beckoned. She raised her face to the sky and ran to greet her vastly changed future.

MARY OF BETHANY

LUKE 10; JOHN 11–12

Mary and her sister Martha's reputation for hospitality was known throughout their village. They delighted in opening their home to passersby in need of food and lodging. The women invited Jesus to stay with them any time He came to Bethany.

Mary delighted in sitting at Jesus' feet and hearing His word—even when Martha needed help with preparing and serving food and the many tasks necessary to keep a household in good order.

Martha loved to have Jesus stay with them, but it meant much extra work. At times she felt overwhelmed by the magnitude of the task she faced. Sometimes Jesus' disciples accompanied Him. Always curious neighbors dropped by. They could not be sent home at meal times for fear of being considered ill-mannered, so they, too, must be fed.

On one such occasion, Martha's resentment rose to a full boil. More than the usual number of guests had appeared, and where was Mary when most needed? Where else? Sitting at the Master's feet, listening to His words.

A pang went through Martha, and a lump formed in her throat. If only she could also sit at the Master's feet and hear what He said. Why didn't Mary realize the burden she placed on her sister? Why didn't she offer to take her place supervising the endless chores, the roasting and baking, breadmaking and serving? A little voice inside reminded her she wasn't being fair. Mary did her share of cooking and cleaning. She just couldn't bear to be out of Jesus' sight when He came, even to help with the serving.

"Suppose I just walked away from my tasks and joined her?" Martha muttered. "Fine thing. None would be given food or drink until their bellies loudly protested."

Cumbered about with much serving, Martha came to Jesus. "Lord, dost Thou not care that my sister hath left me to serve alone? Bid her therefore that she help me."

Mary rose, a stricken look on her face. It was always thus. She became so engrossed in the Master's words as He spoke with her brother Lazarus and others who gathered, she forgot her duties. Like a child, she stood with bowed head and quivering lips. What must Jesus think of her? She scarcely dared raise her head enough to look at either Him or Martha.

Jesus hesitated a long moment. He sighed and spoke in a voice that held more sadness than condemnation. "Martha, Martha," He said. "Thou art careful and troubled about many things—"

Mary saw the pleased look creep over her sister's face. Such was high praise from the Master. But why did He address Martha, instead of her slothful sister?

Mary held her breath and Jesus continued.

"One thing is needful; and Mary hath chosen that good part, which shall not be taken away from her."

The constricting bands about Mary's heart loosened at His words. She caught quick tears in Martha's eyes, the look of shame at having complained. Martha looked cut to the quick.

Tenderhearted Mary sprang to her sister's side. She wrapped her arms around Martha. "I will help you," she promised. "Then we both shall sit at Jesus' feet."

Readers of the Mary and Martha story often dwell on Jesus' rebuke to Martha and praise of Mary. Yet Jesus did not consider Martha a bad person. On the other hand, He freely praised her for being "careful and troubled about many things." When He pointed out one thing was needed in her life, it didn't mean for her to give up doing the daily chores that require attention. Jesus well knew the necessity of hard labor from lessons learned at Joseph's knee in the carpenter shop and from watching His mother perform household duties.

In saying Mary had chosen that good part that would not be taken from her, Jesus wanted Martha to focus on what was even more important. He would not always abide in the home at Bethany. Martha must learn to store up His teachings, as Mary did, against the time of His departure. Everyday duties would always abound. The opportunity for the sisters to hear Him would not.

MARTHA

LUKE 10; JOHN 11–12

Lazarus lay ill, little caring or responding to his sisters' tender ministrations. In spite of everything they could do, he grew worse. Martha and Mary called a servant and ordered, "Go to Jesus and say unto Him, 'Lord, behold, he whom thou lovest is sick.'" They watched the servant hasten to obey, a measure of comfort stealing into their hearts. In a short time, Jesus would come, and all would be well.

Minutes dragged into anxious hours, but Jesus did not come. "Did you not make clear how sick Lazarus is?" Martha demanded of the servant.

"Yea, mistress."

"Then why does He not come?" she cried. "It has been two days."

Lower and lower Lazarus sank until no life remained in him. Martha and Mary could not understand why Jesus tarried along the way. They sadly prepared their brother for burial, hot tears falling on the linen wrappings. They laid him to rest in a cave and rolled a stone before it. The entire household went into mourning for the brother and master who would be with them no more.

"Jesus could have saved Lazarus," Martha bitterly told Mary.

"I know." Her sister sighed, eyes filled with trouble.

Many of the Jews came to comfort the bereaved women. Days later, word came that Jesus was nigh unto Bethany. Martha laid aside her tasks and hurried to meet Him, but Mary sat still in the house. When Martha reached Jesus she burst into tears. "Lord, if Thou hadst been here, my brother had not died. But I know, that even now, whatsoever Thou wilt ask of God, God will give it Thee."

Jesus said unto her, "Thy brother shall rise again."

"I know." Martha sobbed, desolate at the loss of the brother she loved and had cared for so long. "He shall rise again in the resurrection at the last day."

"I am the resurrection, and the life; he that believeth in Me, though he were dead, yet shall he live: And whosoever liveth and believeth in Me shall never die. Believest thou this?"

All Jesus' teachings rushed back to confirm the truth to the sorrowful woman. She cried in a voice that held not only faith but knowledge. "Yea, Lord: I believe that Thou art the Christ, the Son of God, which should come into the world." Then she went back to the house and whispered to Mary, "The Master is come, and calleth for thee."

Jesus had not yet entered the town. When the Jews saw Mary rise up and go to meet Him, they murmured, "She goeth unto the grave to weep," and followed her, as did Martha.

Mary reached Jesus and fell at His feet. "Lord, if Thou hadst been here, my brother had not died."

Jesus groaned in the spirit and was troubled. "Where have ye laid him?"

The Jews said, "Lord, come and see."

Jesus wept, and the Jews murmured among themselves, "Behold how He loved him!" But some said, "Could not this man, which opened the eyes of the blind, have caused that even this man should not have died?"

Martha's broken heart echoed the question over and over as she stumbled after Jesus on the way to the grave.

"Take ye away the stone," Jesus commanded.

"Lord, by this time he stinketh: For he hath been dead four days."

Jesus told her, "Said I not unto thee, that, if thou wouldst believe, thou shouldest see the glory of God?" Martha didn't understand and shrank back when the stone, with much grinding, moved away from the grave.

Jesus prayed to His Father in heaven, then cried in a loud voice, "Lazarus, come forth." Martha gasped and huddled close to Mary. The watching Jews stood as if frozen. A white figure appeared, bound hand and foot with graveclothes and face covered with a napkin. "Loose him and let him go," Jesus ordered. In fear and trembling, it was done. Lazarus stood before them, strong, whole, resurrected from the dead.

With one accord, those present fell to the ground. They rubbed their eyes, unable to believe what they saw. Many of the Jews who came to comfort Mary and Martha and had seen the things Jesus did believed on Him from that day.

It is interesting to note that Martha, once gently reproved by the Master, showed such strong faith that she cried affirmation from the midst of tragedy. Out of a broken heart came her unshakable belief in the resurrection.

Too often Martha is remembered as a woman so busy with household duties she didn't take time to listen to Jesus. She should be remembered for her valiant testimony that Jesus was the Son of God.

ZACCHAEUS

LUKE 19:1–10

This little man had a big job: He was chief tax collector in Jericho. This made him both rich and despised because he collected taxes from the common people to give to Rome. Yet even he was interested in the famous teacher and healer from Nazareth.

Jesus was coming into the city. Zaccheus struggled to catch a glimpse of him through the throng of people. But he was too short to see anything. So he ran ahead of the procession and climbed up a sycamore tree beside the road. From here he could see everyone—and everyone could see him.

Jesus stopped beneath the tree. "Come down, Zaccheus," the Master called. "I'm coming to stay at your house today."

The crowd thought it strange that Jesus would associate with someone they considered a sinner. But while Jesus was at his house Zaccheus changed their minds. He announced he would give half his possessions to the poor and return four times the amount of money he had collected dishonestly.

"Salvation has come to this house today," Jesus said and reminded His critics, "I came to seek and to save those who are lost."

THE WOMAN AT THE WELL

JOHN 4

The Samaritan woman turned slow steps toward Jacob's well. She hated going there. Her neighbors pulled their skirts aside when she passed by and murmured against her. Yet she must have water if she was to live, and the sixth hour was as good a time to draw water as any.

Raising her head, she noted a man sitting nearby. He looked tired. His garments showed him to be a Jew. Dread filled her. It was bad enough being the object of scorn among her own kind, but the smug, self-righteous Jews who came to the well as they passed through Samaria made her feel less than the dirt beneath their sandals. She silently stepped forward to draw water so she could leave at once. A pleasant voice halted her, saying, "Give me to drink."

She looked full in his face, and her lips curled. "How is it that thou, being a Jew, askest drink of me, which am a woman of Samaria? for the Jews have no dealings with the Samaritans." If the stranger had the brains of a donkey he would know this and not have to be told.

"If thou knewest the gift of God, and who it is that saith to thee, give me to drink; thou wouldest have asked of him, and he would have given thee living water," he told her.

Living water? Amazed at his manner of speaking she retorted, "Sir, thou hast nothing to draw with, and the well is deep: from whence then hast thou that living water? Art thou greater than our father Jacob, which gave us the well, and drank thereof himself, and his children, and his cattle?"

Jesus told her whoever drank water from Jacob's well thirsted again, but those who drank of the water He would give should never thirst. He said, "The water that I give him shall be in him a well of water springing up into everlasting life."

Why should the strange words churn her spirit? Suppose this magician could give her water so she never again had to thirst or to come to the well and draw? She impulsively pleaded with Him to do so, but Jesus bade her to go, call her husband, and come back to the well.

Shame reddened her face, and she cast her gaze downward to escape His piercing look. "I have no husband." To her amazement, He responded she had spoken well, for although she had had five husbands, the man she now had was not her husband.

Fear came upon her. "Sir, I perceive that Thou art a prophet."

He expounded many things to her. With each truth, her spirit kindled until it flamed into response. "I know that Messias cometh, which is called Christ: When He is come, He will tell us all things."

Jesus said, "I that speak unto thee am He."

The woman straightway left her waterpot. She raced to the city and said unto the men, "Come, see a man which told me all things that ever I did: Is not this the Christ?" She ran to others, proclaiming what had come to pass that day to all who would listen. They went out of the city and came unto Him. Many believed on Him by reason of the woman's testimony. They besought Him to tarry, and Jesus abode there two days.

Many more believed because of Jesus' own word, for they had heard Him themselves and knew He was indeed the Christ, the Savior of the world. The Samaritan woman found a niche in history because she listened, believed, and shouted the truth of Jesus, the Christ, through the streets of her city.

THE WOMAN ACCUSED

JOHN 8

The wretched woman brought to the temple by the scribes and Pharisees dared not raise her head, yet in spite of her terror, she felt a certain sense of release. Today would end her miserable life. If it wasn't for the agony to come with the sharp stones hurled by men no better than she, she wouldn't care. Perhaps the gods would be merciful and allow the first to stun or fell her with a blow to the head.

"Master, this woman was taken in adultery, in the very act. Now Moses in the law commanded us that such should be stoned: But what sayest Thou?"

A long stillness followed, so lengthy the accused woman risked a quick glance at the teacher someone in the crowd had addressed as Jesus. He looked kinder than those who had taken her, but it would avail nothing. A law was a law, not to be broken. She thought bitterly of the man with whom she had been found. Why was he not here, as well? Had those who took her conveniently allowed him to escape?

The silence continued, then a slight rustling sound came from Jesus' robe as He stooped down and with His finger wrote on the ground, as though He heard them not.

The prisoner wondered, but the scribes and Pharisees continued railing against her, demanding that Jesus answer.

He raised up and said unto them, "He that is without sin among you, let him first cast a stone at her." He stooped down again and wrote upon the ground.

The woman's mouth fell open. Little as she knew about Jewish law, she realized Jesus had challenged those who brought her to be judged with the sharpest challenge imaginable. Not that it would benefit her. Some of these self-righteous men considered themselves so holy they wouldn't recognize sin in their hearts if it stung like the desert scorpions.

She tensed, waiting for the first missile to tear into her flesh. Someone coughed. Feet shuffled. She felt movement and raised her head. Jesus still stooped down, busy with writing, but one by one, the scribes and Pharisees stole away.

At last, Jesus arose and faced her. "Woman, where are those thine accusers? hath no man condemned thee?"

Trembling, unable to believe she alone remained before Jesus, she stammered, "No man, Lord."

He looked straight into her eyes. She felt He knew everything about her, more than anyone on earth could know. He spoke. "Neither do I condemn thee: Go, and sin no more."

When Jesus had gone, she stood alone in the place where her huddled, broken body would have lain if not for Him, still dazed from the strange encounter with even stranger results. Instead of a death sentence, Jesus had given pardon and an admonition: Go, and sin no more.

What lay ahead? New life, surely. For once she looked into Jesus' face and beheld His majesty, the past meant nothing; the future, everything.

A DESPERATE MOTHER

JOHN 9

Each time her son went forth to beg, his mother's heart ached. Was it not enough that God had cursed him with blindness from birth? Why must he also be forced to beg? She sighed. There was no other choice. She and her husband between them could not earn enough to provide even the rudest shelter, the coarsest food without the pittance the son brought in.

"Better to die and be out of this miserable life," she muttered.

Strange tales came to their household of a teacher said to heal. Neighbors told stories passed on from those who claimed to have stood by and seen Jesus of Nazareth touch the infirm and make them whole. Something stirred within the blind man's mother. She hastily pressed it down. Even Jehovah did not heal those blind from birth. Yet her gnarled hands stilled at her work, and she caught herself dreaming. Suppose. . .

"Nay," she chastised herself. "Such a thing cannot be, although I am desperate enough to try anything. Perhaps I should seek out this teacher and see for myself if He does the miracles they say."

One day she went to the place where her son sat begging. A little crowd had gathered in front of the spot her son occupied. The mother heard someone ask, "Master, who did sin, this man, or his parents, that he was born blind?"

Anguish went through the listening mother. Had she not asked herself the same question as many times as there were stars in the sky? She numbly waited for the answer that would confirm and condemn her.

A rich voice replied, one filled with compassion and authority. "Neither hath this man sinned, nor his parents: But that the works of God should be made manifest in him. . ."

The woman elbowed her way through a resentful crowd until she stood near her son. She watched the man whose back was to her stoop, spit on the ground, and make clay of the spittle and dirt.

She gasped when He anointed the eyes of her blind son and commanded, "Go, wash in the pool of Siloam."

Paralyzed by shock, the mother saw her son struggle to his feet. She watched him make his way to the pool. He splashed water on his face, removing the last bits of clay clinging to his eyes. The next instant a shriek rose to the heavens. "I see!" He leaped in his gladness. "Praise God, I can see!" He ran toward home on feet made fleet by joy.

When his mother arrived, panting from her exertion, her son stood in a circle of neighbors babbling questions, wondering if this was really he who had been blind. The seeing man told what had happened, yet some could not believe this, their neighbor, had received sight. "Where is the one who healed you?" they asked, but the son knew not.

"My son!" His sobbing mother clasped him in her arms, feeling her bitterness vanish when their tears mingled. It gave her strength to face the Pharisees when they came claiming Jesus was a sinner and not of God. Had He not healed on the Sabbath? They did not believe the man had ever been blind. "Is this your son, who ye say was blind? how then doth he now see?"

The glad mother and father stood their ground, although trembling with fear. These religious leaders had agreed that anyone who confessed Jesus was Christ should be put out of the synagogue. They told the questioners their son had indeed been born blind. They could not explain why he now saw. "He is of age; ask him: He shall speak for himself," they told the Pharisees.

Their son reminded them God did not hear sinners; if Jesus were not of God, He could do nothing. The Pharisees cast him out, still mumbling against Jesus, but the little family rejoiced at the restoring of their son.

Jesus later came to the man He had healed. The son believed and worshipped Him. Did the desperate mother and her husband also accept Him as the Son of God? Perhaps, for Jesus healed far more than their son as He passed by.

LAZARUS

JOHN 11:1–45; 12:1–11, 17–19

Others had performed miracles, but no one except the prophets Elijah and Elisha had ever been known to bring the dead back to life. Yet Jesus knew it was not yet time for His friend Lazarus to leave this world.

Lazarus was a brother of Jesus' followers Mary and Martha. He lived in Bethany. When Jesus heard that Lazarus had become gravely ill, He said that His friend had merely fallen asleep. But Lazarus was indeed dead. He had lain inside a tomb for four days by the time Jesus and His followers drew near Bethany. "If You had been here, he would not have died," Martha and Mary grieved, coming out to meet Jesus.

"He will live again," Jesus said.

He asked to be taken to the cave where Lazarus was entombed. "Remove the stone," He commanded.

"But he'll be smelling awful," Martha gasped. "He's been dead four days!"

"Believe, and you will see the glory of God," Jesus told her. When the stone had been moved, Jesus prayed aloud that God would perform a miracle so the people would know that He was God's Son. Then He called into the cave, "Lazarus, come out!"

The man who had died emerged, bound in burial clothes from head to toe.

As a result of Lazarus's resurrection, many doubters started to believe Jesus indeed was the Messiah. This frightened Jesus' opponents and accelerated their efforts to have Him killed.

STEPHEN

ACTS 6:5–8:2

He had a face like an angel as the false case was brought against him. Stephen, chosen to serve the church in Jerusalem, was charged with preaching against the law of Moses and against God. In reality, Stephen possessed special God-given powers to perform miracles and to speak with wisdom in the name of Christ. He was such an effective speaker that his critics were unable to argue with him. So they plotted lies against him and brought him before the high priest.

When he was asked to defend himself, Stephen spoke eloquently of how God had guided their ancestors. He reminded his listeners how the people of old had revolted against their leader Moses and had angered the Lord by worshipping an idol. He concluded by boldly charging his accusers with breaking Moses' law themselves—and of murdering the Lamb of God, Jesus Christ.

This infuriated them. They became so angry they ground their teeth and covered their ears so they could no longer hear Stephen. A maddened, unreasonable mob finally rushed and seized Stephen.

The brave disciple seemed oblivious to the uproar around him. He lifted his eyes and gazed on a most beautiful vision: the Son of man, Jesus Christ, standing at the right side of God.

Stephen described what he saw to his tormentors, but it only angered them further. They hustled him outside the city and began throwing rocks at him. Under the deadly barrage, Stephen asked God to receive his spirit. As he fell to his knees, he cried out—as his Savior on the cross had cried out not long before—"Lord, do not count this sin against them." Then he died.

Thus Stephen became the first martyr for Christ. Among the throng of killers was a young man named Saul who became the most dreaded persecutor of the early church—until his own encounter with the Lord changed him into a steadfast, unflinching Christian martyr like his forerunner, Stephen.

PAUL

ACTS 7:57–28:30; THE LETTERS OF PAUL

When Stephen, the first Christian martyr, was stoned to death in Jerusalem, a young man named Saul kept the coats of the men who attacked him. Saul then joined the general effort to eradicate Christ's disciples and became one of the leading persecutors of the early church. He went from house to house, arrested the believers, and threw them in jail.

The Jewish leaders sent Saul to Damascus to arrest Christ's followers there. But on the way Saul met Jesus. This would have enormous impact on the spread of Christianity.

On the road to Damascus, the Lord appeared to Saul and his companions as a blinding light. "Why are you persecuting Me?" a voice demanded.

"Who are You?" Saul asked.

"It is I, Jesus, the One you are persecuting."

Blinded and trembling, Saul asked, "What do You want me to do?"

Jesus told him to go into Damascus and wait for instructions there.

Meanwhile the Lord told a believer in Damascus named Ananias to find Saul. Ananias was hesitant because he'd heard of Saul's merciless persecution of the Christians. But he did as God told him.

When Ananias touched Saul, scales fell from the tormentor's eyes so he could see again. Right away, Saul was baptized and filled with the Holy Spirit; he joined the believers in Damascus, and began preaching with power that astonished the hearers. They knew he'd come to Damascus as an enemy of Christ, not a believer. Not only so, the Jewish leaders there conspired to kill him. But his Christian friends smuggled him out of the city hidden in a large basket.

Saul returned to Jerusalem. At first, he was rejected by the Christians because of his reputation. They doubted that their former persecutor had sincerely believed in Christ. But through the mediation of a church leader named Barnabas, Saul was accepted and began to help build up the young church. Again the Jewish leaders tried to kill him, and again his new Christian comrades whisked him away to safety.

Saul became a missionary and soon after became known as Paul. He and his companions traveled through the Roman Empire preaching the gospel, encouraging new believers, and teaching the young churches how to worship and conduct their lives as believers. Paul and his companions were the objects of harassment and imprisonment and ultimately were executed for their beliefs. This was a complete role reversal for the one-time persecutor named Saul.

In his journeys through the eastern Mediterranean, Paul lived in constant danger from the Lord's foes and from the uncertainties of travel. Not only was he shipwrecked, he was jailed and often beaten.

Even in captivity Paul was a powerful witness for Christ. Once Paul and his companion Silas were imprisoned in Philippi because they freed a slave girl from an evil spirit of fortune-telling. Her owners were furious with Paul and Silas because the owners had been using her fortune-telling as a means of making money. They convinced the court to imprison Paul.

Stripped and severely beaten, Paul and Silas were chained deep inside the prison. There, in the middle of the night, the apostles prayed and sang hymns to the other prisoners! Next, God sent an earthquake that shook the prison so violently that the heavy doors fell open and the chains were loosened from the inmates. When the jailer ran to investigate, he thought the prisoners had escaped. The Romans would kill him for this! He was about to commit suicide when Paul stopped him. "Don't worry," Paul told him, "we are all here." The jailer and his entire household believed in Jesus as a result of this event.

Paul was finally sent to Rome for a trial before Caesar Nero. While awaiting trial, Paul continued to preach the gos-pel for two years while living in a rented house. Scripture does not record his end, but it's assumed that Paul was beheaded in Rome before Nero fell from power in A.D. 68.

RHODA

ACTS 12

Rhoda, who served in the house of Mary, the mother of John Mark, made herself small in the corner and listened to the prayers of those around her.

"We beseech Thee on behalf of our brother Peter," one prayed. "Has not Herod, the king, already killed James, the brother of John? Father, Thou knowest how it pleased those Jews who believe not in Jesus, so much that Herod further took Peter. Even now our beloved brother lies in prison, guarded by many soldiers. Deliver him, O God, that he may bring us Thy word again."

Rhoda fought back tears. She loved the big, rough man Christ had called from his fishing nets to be a fisher of men. When he laughed, her own lips curved upwards. Most of all, she loved hearing Peter's stories about Jesus.

If only she, too, could have walked with the Master! Rhoda found it hard to stay with her duties when Peter came. She longed to sit at his feet every waking hour. Each retold tale of the Christ made the young maiden's heart beat faster.

She silently prayed for Peter. She knew although it was simple and short, the petition would mingle with the prayers of the others in a mighty plea to God.

Ears made keen by service detected a knocking at the gate. Rhoda's heart gave a sickening lurch. Since Herod stretched forth his hands to vex certain of the church, believers lived with fear. They refused to give up their beliefs and prayers but knew they, like so many others, might be seized.

On slow feet, the damsel went to the gate. "It is Peter," a voice said.

Relief and joy filled her. So glad was she, Rhoda failed to open the gate, but ran back inside. "Peter even now stands before the gate," she cried.

Disbelief filled their faces. "Thou art mad," they told her.

"Nay," Rhoda insisted again and again. "I did not mistake his voice."

Those in the house looked at one another. "It is his angel."

The knocking increased. At last they opened the door. They gaped in astonishment. Peter stood outside, face creased by a broad smile. He beckoned with his hand for them to hold their peace, then stepped inside.

"I have much to tell you," he said in the mighty voice that once bellowed orders to his fishing comrades during wild storms. "This same night I lay sleeping between two soldiers, bound with two chains. The keepers before the door kept the prison." Excitement and triumph shone in his eyes.

"I awakened when a light shined in the prison; I thought it a vision. A man stood before me. He smote me on the side and raised me up, saying, 'Arise up quickly.' My chains clanked; I felt their weight lift when they fell from me.

"The man told me to gird myself and bind on my sandals. He ordered me to cast my garment about me and follow him. I obeyed. When we were safely past the first and the second ward, we came unto the iron gate that leadeth into the city. I marveled, for it opened to us of its own accord. We went out and passed on through one street. My companion departed." He hesitated.

Rhoda felt her body tremble. She had seen Peter in many dispositions, but never had his countenance shone brighter. She clasped her hands and waited.

Peter's voice dropped to a whisper. A look of awe came to his face. "I came to myself and realized where I was. I cried, 'Now I know of a surety that the Lord hath sent His angel and hath delivered me out of the hand of Herod, and from all the expectation of the people of the Jews.' I came to this house." His eyes twinkled with merriment. "My young sister grew so excited, she left me standing outside the gate."

"In spite of our constant prayers, we did not believe it could really be you," one of the eldest brokenly confessed. "God forgive us! Only this maiden, scarcely past childhood, recognized the truth."

Peter smiled and Rhoda's heart burned within her. She would never forget this night, not even if she lived beyond the allotted three score and ten years* and became an aged, wrinkled crone.

---

*Psalm 90:10

LYDIA

Lydia of the city of Thyatira was known for her successful selling in the marketplace. Word of her dealings in purple cloth brought to her those from many walks of life. She furnished the finest fabrics to some of the most well-known households in the city, royalty included.

Besides having the high degree of business knowledge needed to compete with other sellers of purple, Lydia possessed an ever greater and more precious attribute: She worshipped God.

One Sabbath, she discovered a much discussed preacher named Paul intended to pray and speak to the women of the city by a riverside. "I will see for myself what manner of man Paul—once known as Saul, who sought out and persecuted Christians—really is," she told herself.

Seated among the others who flocked to hear, she felt her heart being opened to Paul's message. It burned within her, and when Paul asked for those who believed to come and be baptized, not only she but her entire household came and entered the waters of the river.

Afterwards, she besought Paul, saying, "If ye have judged me to be faithful to the Lord, come into my house, and abide there."

Paul reports, "She constrained us," meaning him and Timothy.

Imagine Lydia's great joy at having them in her home. What stories she and the faithful members of her household must have heard from the determined Paul who now brought people to Christ even more fervently than he once persecuted them unto death! How many miracles took place within the home she gladly opened to the servant of the Lord? There is no record, but surely the good woman received great blessings in return for her faith and kindness.

TIMOTHY

ACTS 16:1; 17:14–15; 18:5; PHILIPPIANS 1:1; 2:19;
COLOSSIANS 1:1; 1 TIMOTHY; 2 TIMOTHY; HEBREWS 13:23

Timothy was Paul's trusted associate—a remarkable status for a young man. He was among the first Christian missionaries and was in charge of the church in Ephesus on the coast of Asia Minor. Ephesus had been the scene of a major riot when Timothy visited the city with Paul. Like many other leaders of the early church, Timothy endured persecution and imprisonment.

Paul's first letter to Timothy gave advice and instructions on how to lead a church. Paul warned against unsound teachers, discussed the purpose of worship and the necessary qualities of church elders and deacons, admonished Timothy to use his God-given talents, and advised him how to deal with specific problems and circumstances he would face as a church leader. "Don't be self-conscious about your youthfulness," Paul told Timothy. "Just concentrate on setting a good example by what you say, how you live, your love for people, and your faith in God."

Timothy's second letter from Paul was brief and climaxed with Paul's premonition of his martyrdom. "I have fought the good fight," Paul wrote. "I have finished the race. I have kept the faith."

Paul was in Rome awaiting his trial before Nero when he wrote the letters to Timothy. He implored Timothy and the apostle Mark to join him in Rome. And so perhaps Timothy was present at the martyrdom of the apostle Paul, his father in the faith.

Inspirational Library

Beautiful purse/pocket-size editions of Christian classics bound in flexible leatherette. These books make thoughtful gifts for everyone on your list, including yourself!

When I'm on My Knees   The highly popular collection of devotional thoughts on prayer, especially for women.
    Flexible Leatherette. $4.99

The Bible Promise Book   Over 1,000 promises from God's Word arranged by topic. What does God promise about matters like: Anger, Illness, Jealousy, Love, Money, Old Age, and Mercy? Find out in this book!
    Flexible Leatherette. $3.99

Daily Wisdom for Women   A daily devotional for women seeking biblical wisdom to apply to their lives. Scripture taken from the New American Standard Version of the Bible.
    Flexible Leatherette. $4.99

My Daily Prayer Journal   Each page is dated and features a Scripture verse and ample room for you to record your thoughts, prayers, and praises. One page for each day of the year.
    Flexible Leatherette. $4.99

Available wherever books are sold.
Or order from:

Barbour Publishing, Inc.
P.O. Box 719
Uhrichsville, OH 44683
www.barbourbooks.com

If you order by mail, add $2.00 to your order for shipping.
Prices are subject to change without notice.